Astrological Judgement of Diseases from the Decumbiture of the Sick
(1655)

and
Urinalia *(1658)*

by
Nicholas Culpeper

Better books make better astrologers.
Here are some of our other titles:

Christian Astrology, books 1 & 2, *by William Lilly*
Christian Astrology, book 3, *by William Lilly*

Encyclopedia of Astrology, *by Nicholas deVore*

Degrees of the Zodiac Symbolized, *a set by Charubel, another by Sepharial*

An Encyclopaedia of Psychological Astrology, *by C.E.O. Carter*

Encyclopaedia of Medical Astrology, *by H.L. Cornell, M.D.*

Ancient Astrology Theory & Practice: **Matheseos Libri VIII**, *by Firmicus Maternus, translated by Jean Rhys Bram*

Tetrabiblos, *by Ptolemy, translated by J.M. Ashmand*

Electional Astrology, *by Vivian Robson*
Astrology and Sex, *by Vivian Robson*
Fixed Stars & Constellations in Astrology, *by Vivian Robson*

The Astrological Judgement and Practice of Physick, *by Richard Saunders*

Mundane Astrology: *Books by H.S. Green, Raphael & C.E.O. Carter*

Carmen Astrologicum, *by Dorotheus of Sidon, translated by David Pingree*

Horary Astrology, The Art of Astrological Divination, *by Derek Appleby*

If not available from your local bookseller, order directly from:

The Astrology Center of America
207 Victory Lane
Bel Air MD 21014

on the web at:
http://www.astroamerica.com

ASTROLOGICAL JUDGEMENT OF DISEASES

From the Decumbiture of the Sick

much enlarged

From Aven Ezra by way of Introduction.
From Noel Duret by way of Direction

wherein is laid down
The Way and manner of finding out the Cause, Change and End of the disease. Also whether the Sick be likely to live or die; and the Time When a Recovery or Death is to be expected.

With the signs of Life or Death by the body of the Sick party; according to the judgement of Hippocrates.

To which is added A Table of Logistical Logarithymes

By Nicholas Culpeper, Gent.
Student in Physick and Astrologie

London, Printed for Nath. Brookes at the Golden Angel on Cornhill, near the Exchange, 1655

Astrology Classics

On the cover:
Anatomical Study *by Leonardo da Vinci*

ISBN: 1 933303 04 2

Published 2003 by:
Astrology Classics
The publication division of

The Astrology Center of America
207 Victory Lane
Bel Air MD 21014

on the web at
http://www.astroamerica.com

NICHOLAS CULPEPER,
Born Oct.18. 11 in. P.M.
1616.

TO THE
ASTROLOGICAL
PHYSITIANS
OF
ENGLAND
NICHOLAS CULPEPER

wisheth peace and prosperity
in this World, and eternal
beatitude **in that which** is to come

THE STATIONER to the Reader:

Courteous Reader,

It is not unknown with how great applause this book was attended when it was first made publick. For it overcame the envy of malicious tongues with the general good it brought, in disclosing even to mean capacities the rarest and deepest mysteries of Physick, which till now were concealed and lockt up in unknown Languages; without the assistance of large commendations advancing its own reputation, and the perfection of that most noble Science. Which when the Author saw so wel approved by men of judgement, he was not a little encouraged to take it to a second review, that he might not only reforme the errours which easily might be overslipt in the heat of the first composure, but also enrich it with Annotations & additions of his own. But ere he could perform this, Death took him away, leaving none to perfect what he had begun, and few who with that diligence and industry endeavoured to be more accomplisht either in the speculation or the practice of what he professed. Yet being unwilling that so good a work should die with him, he entrusted his papers with some of his nearest friends to be Published with those Experiences which he was forced to leave behind him. Thus at length they came to our hands, and not till at length; which was the reason that for a time we frustrated not only our own promises, but deceived the expectations of other men. But Otis hoped, Courteous Reader, that now you know the cause of the delay, you will easily grant our pardon, and accept rather late, then never, this Legacy of a dying man, bequeathed to you upon his death-bed on the confidence of his former practise and experience.

Yours, Nath. BROOK.

Dear Souls,

To you all, and to you especially that heard these lectures do I dedicate them, and present them to you not to look upon onely (for then I had as good have sent you a picture, and as much it would have pleased your eye) Man was made not onely for speculation, but also for practice; speculation brings only pleasure to a man's self; it's practice which benefits others. And I hope I need not tell you that man was not born for himself alone. These Rules will serve (if heedfully observed by the eye of Reason) to ballance your judgment in fayling through the Prognostical part of Physick, that so you may steer your course by the Card of Truth, and not float unsettledly upon the waves of Errour, Ignorance or Opinion. To you (rather then any that I know) belongs the practice of Physick; & that practice may be perfect, Judgement ought to be sound; and to make judgement sound, is required an exquisite knowledge. Judgement is perfected by knowledge, knowledge by experience; whence it appears the more communicative knowledge is, so much more excellent it is. Of all the men in the world I hate a drone most, that sucks the sweetnesse of other mens labours, but doth no good himself; and will as soon teach Physick or Astrology to an Oak, as to a creature, the center of whose actions is terminated in himself. Surely, surely, if God had not made the nature of man communicative, he would not have made one man to stand in continual need of another: but we see the contrary, and the sons of wisdom know how to pick out the meaning of God from it.

I have given you here all my Prognosications from the Decumbiture of the sick party; And although I ingenuously confesse the greatest part of them will hold true in a Horarie Question erected upon the sight of the Urine, of which I have now added a compendious Treatise; yet this is my judgement at present, that next the Nativity, the Decumbiture is the safest and surest ground for you to build your judgment upon; and-you shall always find it by experience.

Excellent and true was that Mottoe of HERMES TRISMEGISTUS. QUOD EST SUPERIUS, EST SICUT INFERIUS; and this will appear to the eye of everyone that deserves the name of a reasonable man, if he do but consider,That his body is made of the same materials that the whole Universe is made of, though not in the same form; namely of a composition of contrary elements. There is scarce a man breathing that knowes his right hand from his left, but knows that if you set bottles of hot water to a mans feet, it will make his head sweat; and the reason is, the mutual harmony of one part of the body with another; why then as well should not the actions of one part of the creation produce as well effects in another, that being also one entire body, composed of the same elements, and in as great harmony ? What's the reason that a man will do more for his brother than he will for a stranger ? is it not because he is formed by the blood of the same mother, & begotten by the seed of the same father ? why then should not the Celestial bodies act upon the Terrestriall, they being made of the same matter, and by the finger of the same God. He that will not believe reason, let him believe Experience; lie that will believe neither, is little better then an Infidel. I confess this way of Judicature Bath been desired by many, promised by some, but hitherto performed by none; which was the motive cause I then took the task in hand myself, which I have now enlarged. In performing whereof, in many places I correcting the faylings of my Author. What was frivolous I left out, as being unwilling to blot paper, and trouble your brains with impertinencies: where lie was too large, I abbreviated him; and where he was deficient, I supplied him both with Precept and example. If there be any failings, consider

1- NEMOSINE CRIMINE VIVIT
That Man nev'r breathed yet, Nor ever shall,
That did all well, and had no fault at all.

2. My Failings (if any be) were not intentional, but accidental: together with this Astrological Judgement, I have also given you the judgement of HIPPOCRATES, & Others. The rules whereof are drawn from the person of the sick; which although they have been printed before, yet I have compared them with the original copy, and brought them into a plainer method, so that you may have your desire at one single ingress. If you make use of both these waies together in judging the disease, without a miracle you can hardly fail. If any find fault with the shortnesse of my rules, let them learn to walk worthy of those they have first; their own experience will bring them more; he's but an apish Physitian that builds all his practice upon other mens foundations. Man was born to look after knowledge, and in this particular you are set in the way how to find it, by one that desires to be a friend to all honest and ingenuous Arts.

Thus have you what I have done, and you know for whose sake I did it. What now remains, but that you labor with might and main for you own good, and the increase of your own knowledge to make experience of them ? For as the diligent hand maketh rich, so the diligent mind encreaseth knowledge; and for my own particular, never fear, but during the time I am amongst the living, I shall never cease to do you good in what way I may or can'

Spittlefields,
Next door to the
Red Lyon

Nich. CULPEPER.

Horoscopes of Notable Astrologers
No VI
Nicholas Culpepper

(Author of the "Herbal", "The Physical Dispensatory", and many other works.)

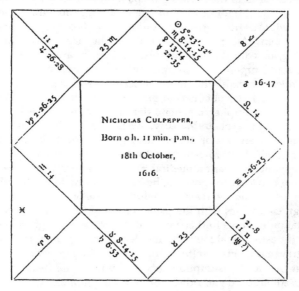

NICHOLAS CULPEPPER,
Born o h. 11 min. p.m.,
18th October,
1616.

⊙ ☍ ♄ , ∠ ♂
☽ ☍ ♃ , ∠ ♄ △ ☿
☿ △ ☽ ✶ ♃
♀ ✶ ♂ (? △ ♅)
♂ ✶ ♀ ∠ ⊙
♃ ✶ ☿ ☍ ☽
♄ ∠ ☽

♅ approximate place is near cusp of the sixth in ♊
♄ ⊙ ♀ ⊙R♄☿ ☿ angular, and
♃ dignified in ♐.

THE above horoscope is taken from Sibly's Illustration of the Occult Sciences. As Will be seen his significator is Saturn, posited on the cusp of the fourth angle in semi-square aspect to the Moon in sixth. At the time Sibly published his work, the planet Herschel or Uranus, had not been discovered, and if my surmise is correct, his position is about the cusp of the sixth house, and furnishes a "key" to the nativity. As most people know, he compiled a "herbal" bearing his Name, and his successor's, in a greater or lesser degree, have largely copied from his work. He was a clever Astrologer, note Mercury, the strongest planet in the figure, in the Mid-heaven, in the occult sign Scorpio in trine to the Moor and sextile to Jupiter, besides the Sun and Venus (the latter trine to Uranus) being also in the same sign. The testimonies for a medical career, and the honor and reputation arising therefrom, are likewise deduced from the sign on the mid-heaven, and the planets therein. All persons who have this sign ascending, culminating, or who (have many planets therein, are inclined to medicine and surgery, but in this case it will be noticed that Mercury rules the sixth, (the house of sickness) and is in the tenth denoting honor to be obtained in matters connected with it, also gain therefrom, as Jupiter, a general significator of wealth, is in his own sign (♐) in sextile to Mercury. His methods of investigation and treatment were out of the ordinary groove, for if Herschel is on crisp of sixth, he throws a trine to the mid-heaven, and thus brings originality to bear on medical treatment, and if I am correct in assuming this to be his position, he has (according to many) rule over the second house (wealth), which he obtained, and as a "fixed" sign culminates with the planet of honor (the Sun) therein, his reputation endures to this day, whilst those who laughed and jeered at his astrological methods, are dead and forgotten. He was very extravagant, his brethren of the profession stated his complaint as a "consumption of the purse," he was very kind-hearted but prodigal, vide Moon opposing Jupiter.

It will be seen the Sun is afflicted, and people of position (notably the doctors) were at enmity with him, and as his significator (Saturn) is on cusp of fourth and opposed by the Sun, they did him lasting damage. There is a deal of mild sarcasm in his writings, especially when quoting "Doctor Reason and Doctor Experience," which may emanate from Mars semi-square Sun. I judge his honor was greviously affected as Venus in Scorpio is aspected by Mars, as the influence is by a sextile, I conclude it did no great damage, but I have but little opinion of Venus in this sigh of the Zodiac. I must now leave this very interesting natus, as space allotted to me is limited, I therefore leave it for the student's further investigation.

TABLE OF CONTENTS

Chapter XVI
Containing certain Observations taken out of Cardan, and other expert Physicians.

Presages of life and death by the Body of the Patient being sick...133
Chapter I
Chapter II
Chapter III
Chapter IV
Chapter V
Chapter VI
Chapter VII
Chapter VIII
Chapter IX

The Second Book of the Presages of HIPPOCRATES, you shall find marshalled in this order.
Chapter I
Chapter II
Chapter III
Chapter IV

URINALIA, 165

Chapter I
Of pissing blood..166

Chapter II
Of Inflammation in the Reins..167

Chapter III
Of the Stone in the Reins..169

Chapter IV
Of unmeasurable pissing...171

Chapter V
Of Ulcers in the Reins...172

Chapter VI
Of the Stone in the Bladder...174

Chapter VII
Of blood curdled in the bladder...175

Chapter VIII
Inflammation of the Bladder..176

Chapter IX
Of Ulcers in the Bladder..177

Chapter X
Of the Strangury...178

Chapter XI
Of difficulty of Urine..179

Chapter XII
Of stoppage in the Urine...180

Chapter XIII
Of Ulcers in the Yard..181

I promised a Table of explanation of some hard words in one place of the book; but having looked over the book, I can find none but those at that place which can exceed almost the meanest capacity

The words are these three, Uvula, Gargareon, Columella; the signification of them is all one: I shall tell you:

1. What its substance and place is
2. What its uses are.

1. The Uvula, Gargareon or Columella, chuse you whether, is a red spungy piece of flesh sticking to the roof of the mouth near the throat.

2. Its uses are,
    1. To give pleasantness to the voice, therefore in hoarseness this is afflicted.
    2. To stay the air that it passes not too fast upon the lungs; therefore such as have gotten colds cannot sing well.
    3. It hinders drink, and such liquid things as we eat, from coming out at our noses.

Yours,

NICH. CULPEPER

SEMIOTICA URANIA
OR

Culpeper's
JUDGEMENT OF DISEASES MUCH ENLARGED
Abraham Avenezra

OF CRITICAL DAYS

Lib. 1

It is a palpable and apparent truth that God carries men to the Principles of grace by the Book of the Creatures; For this beginning of **ABRAHAM AVENEZRA** an Arabian Physitian, and a singular Astrologer (whom the Priests of our times call Heathen) favoureth of the things beyond Heathenism; for in this Treatise of CRITICAL DAYS, he begins thus;

I entreat the Lord God, that he would enlighten my heart with his light and truth, so long as my spirit remains in me, for his light is very delightful and good for the eye of my soul to see by; for so shall the night be enlightened to me as the day, neither shall the clouds shadow it; it shall not be like the light of the Sun by day, because it shall not be clouded; nor like the light of the Moon, because it shall never be diminished as her light is. God hath made these lights as he hath made man, and he appointed the greater light to rule the day, and the lesser to rule the night; Hence it appears the Sun was made to rule the day, and not to give light to it only, as the Priests affirm; and the Moon was made to rule the night, not to give light to it onely, as appears Gen. 1 because she hath no light to give; also he hash made the whole host of Heaven, the fixed Stars and Planets, and gave them vertues, **together with the Luminaries; but** their vertues are not so great as the vertues of the Luminaries; **neither is the vertue of the Moon so great as the vertue** the Sun, because she borrows her light from the Sun; also the whole host of Heaven, that is, the fixed Stars, move all in the same Sphere; and therefore their distance is always the same the one from the other, and their latitude is always the same; **but it is not** so with the Planets; for their course is various, and so is their distance the one from the other, and so is their latitude; for sometimes they are upon the Ecliptick, sometimes North from it, sometimes South, sometimes Retrograde, sometimes direct, sometimes in conjunction one with another, sometimes in opposition, sometimes in other aspects; the reason of this is, because the Sphere of one is lower then the Sphere of the other, and the lower the Sphere is, the sooner they make their revolution.

The nearest to the earth of all the Planets is the Moon, and therefore her course is swiftest; and besides her difference in Longitude and Latitude, there happen other accidents to her which are not visible to other Planets; for sometimes she encreaseth, sometimes decreaseth, and sometimes she is invisible or faileth in light; the reason why the Planets are not seen horned as the Moon, is, because their distance is greater from us; all the Planets seem biggest when they are at their greatest distance from the Sun, or when they are nearest the Earth, according to COPERNICUS; also sometimes the Moon is Eclipsed, but not in the same manner as the Sun; for the Sun never loseth its light, but is onely one shadowed from a particular people or place, by the body of the Moon; but the Moon Eclipsed totally loseth her light; and the reason is, the Sun's light is his own, but the Moon is a borrowed light.

This being premised, consider that all things under the Moon universally, whether men, beasts, or plants, are changed, and never remain in the same state, neither are their thoughts and deeds the same; take counsel of your head, and it will certifie you what I speak is true, and they are varied according to the various course and disposition of Planets: look upon your own genesis, and you shall find your thought moved to choler, so often as the Moon transits the place where the body or aspect of MARS was in your genesis; and to melancholy when she doth the like to SATURN; the reason is, because the Moon is assimilated to the body of man; whose vertue as well as her light increaseth and diminisheth; for she brings down the vertue of the other Planets to the creatures, and to man if he lives upon the earth.

The Sun causeth heat and cold, day and night, Winter and Summer. When he arrives to the house of his honour or exaltation, to wit ARIES, then the trees spring, living creatures are comforted, the birds sing, the whole creation rejoyceth, and sicknesses in the body shew themselves in their colours; Also when he arrives at his fall, to wit LIBRA, the leaves of the trees fall, all creatures are lumpish, and mourn like the trees in October.

Also another notable experiment is, usually sick people are something eased from midnight to noon, because then the Sun is in the ascending part of Heaven; but they are most troubled when he is descending, that is, from noon to midnight.

The course of the Moon is to be observed in many operations both in the Sea and Rivers, Vegetables, Shel-fishes, as also in the bones and marrow of men, and all creatures; also seed sown at the wain of the Moon grows either not at all, or to no purpose.

Also wise men have experiences. of many vertues of the Stars, and have left them to posterity; and Physitians in old time (when they were minded to be honest) have found out the changes and terminations of diseases by the course of the Moon; Wherefore the 7, 14, 20 or 21, 27, 28, or 29 days of sickness are called CRITICAL DAYS, which cannot he known but by the course of the Moon; for let not your brain rest in the number of the days, because the Moon is sometimes swifter, sometimes slower.
As for such diseases that do not terminate in a moneth (I mean a Lunar moneth) viz. the time the Moon traceth around the Zodiack, which is 27 days, some odd hours,

some few minutes; you must judge of these by the course of the Sun. The day is not called Critical, because it is the seventh day from the decumbiture, as if the vertue lay in the number 7, but because the Moon comes to the Quartile of the place she was in at the decumbiture, it's no matter whether it be a day sooner or later.

When she comes to the opposition of the place she was in at the day of the decumbiture, she makes a second Crisis, the third when she comes to the second quartile, and the fourth when she comes to the place she was in at the decumbiture, and it's well she can make so many.

The reason of the difference of the Moon's motion is the difference of her distance from the Earth; for when the centre of her circle is nearest to the centre of the Earth, she is swift in motion; and hence it comes to pass that sometimes she moves more than 15 degrees in 24 hours, sometimes less than 12, therefore if she be swift in motion, she comes to her own quartile in six days; if slow, not in seven; therefore you must judge according to the motion of the Moon, and not according to the number of days.

Upon a Critical day, if the Moon be well aspected with good Planets, it goes well with the sick; if by ill Planets, it goes ill; but I know you would be resolved in one particular, which is, if the Crisis depend upon the motion of the Moon and her aspect to the Planets, what is the reason, if two men to be taken sick at one and the same time, that yet the Crisis of the one falls out well, and not so the other ?

I answer, The vertue working is changed according to the diversity of the venue receiving; for you all know the Sun makes the Clay hard, and the Wax soft; it makes the Cloth white, and the Dace black; so then, if one be a child whose nature is hot and moist, the other a young man, and the third an old man, the Crisis works diversely in them all because their ages are different.

Secondly, the time of the year carries a great stroke in this business; if it be in the Spring-time, diseases are most obnoxious to a child, because his nature is hot and moist; a disease works most violently with a choleric man in Summer; with a melancholy man in Autumn; with a flegmatick man by reason of age or complexion in Winter. Thirdly, To this I add, suppose at the beginning of a disease the Moon was in the place of MARS, in the genesis whose nature is hot and dry, if the disease be of heat, it mightily aggravates it; not so if it be cold; and you shall seldome find two men that had MARS in the one and the same place in their genesis, fall sick together, and the disease differ neither as the middle nor at the end.

QUESTION. Put the case the age of the people, and the season of the year be the same, and the disease be the same, would the Crisis be the same, yes or no ?

1.   answer thus, Their complexions may be different, the one hot and dry, the other cold and moist: If the diseases be hot and dry, the effect will not be so violent upon a cold and moist body, as it will upon a hot and dry; the fire will soon seize upon that which is hot and dry, then that which is cold and moist.

2.   Imagine the complexions to be the same upon both parties ? I answer,

That it is impossible, there must be some difference upon complexions; for though they may be the same in the universal, yet in particulars there must needs be some difference, by reason of their different dyet, exercise and climate, unless they be born and brought up altogether under one latitude.

3- Let us imagine they be all alike, yet divers things may intervene and alter the Crisis; their nativities may not agree; for example, if the Moon be in the place of SATURN or MARS in the nativity, the disease is dangerous: not so if she be in the place where JUPITER or VENUS was in then; or it's possible JUPITER or VENUS may hurt in the nativities of such to whose ascendants they are inimical or posited in the sixth or eighth houses.

4   Again, SATURN may be Lord of the one nativity, and not of the other; and then he may hurt the one and not the other, whose nativity he is Lord of; for the Divel will not hurt his own; the like of MARS.

Innumerable such things may be added, as that the one may provide for the sicknesse beforehand, not the other, but it is needless.

OBJECTION. But then you will say there can be no certainty at all found in the Crisis ?

I answer, Astrologers pass judgement two manner of ways in diseases.

The first we call Universal, and so SATURN rules Consumptions, MARS feavers, VENUS over women, MERCURY over Schollars, &c.

The Second is particular, and the Seventh house hath dominion over women, the Ninth over Schollars, &c.

Now no particular can destroy an universal; for example, if VENUS be ill seated in a nativity, and Lord of the Seventh well seated, we say the native shall generally incur evil by women, though some particular good may incur from them; in like manner judge in this case by the general significators of sickness, viz. SATURN and MARS.

But Secondly, if you can possibly get the nativities, you shall not erre; and now give me leave to quote one experiment of my own. If the Nativities be one and the same; the Crisis will be one and the same; For example, I know three Children born at one and the same time (as the event proved): at five years of age they all three had convulsions, whereby they were all three lame of one leg, the boys on the right leg and the girl on the left; at 14 years of age they died altogether in one and the same day of the small pox.

Thirdly, if the Nativity cannot be gotten, view the urine, and erect a celestial Scheme upon the sight of it, and if you have the decumbiture, compare the decumbiture with the celestial Scheme at the view of the urine, and you may judge clearly of the Crisis.

Liber I

To proceed to the matter, if the Moon be strong when she comes to the Quartile, or opposition of the place she was in at the decumbiture, viz. in her house of exultation, the sick recovers, if she be aspected to no Planet.

Judge the like of the Sun in Chronical diseases, but judge the contrary if either of them be in the detriment or falls, for there is as much difference between them as there is between the Zenith and the Nadir: if the Moon be void of course at the beginning of a disease, the sign is neither good nor bad. Look then to the sign ascending at the beginning of a disease, and let the Moon alone for a time.

If the Moon be angular at the decumbiture and in the Ascendant, judge of her alone, and make use of no other significator; if she be not so, joyn the Lord of the Ascendant with her in your judgement.

'Tis very dangerous when the Moon is Eclipsed, when she comes to the quartile or opposition of the place she was in at the decumbiture, for usually at such a time death turns Physitian.

If in the beginning of a sickness the Moon be in a moveable sign, the sickness soon moves to an end one way or other; fixed signs prolong sickess, and common signs set a stop to the wisest brain in the world.

Also this is a certain rule, as sure as the Sun is up at noon day, that diseases of plenitude are very dangerous when a man is taken sick upon a full Moon. Diseases of fasting or emptiness are very dangerous, when a man is taken sick upon a new Moon. Let me entreat you to give Physick for a disease of emptiness when she is near the Full. And for diseases of fullness when the Moon hath lost her light.

Diminish a humour when-- the Moon diminisheth In light; Increase when she increaseth in light; Flegm opposeth Choler, Melancholy opposeth Blood;

'Tis none of the worst ways to diminish choler by increasing flegm; a word is enough to the wise.

'Tis very bad when in the beginning of a sickness the Moon is in a sign of the nature of the humour offending. Naturally when she is in a fiery sign, amend a disease of flegm; but if choler abound, 'tis very good if she be in a watery sign; you may know by a penny how a shilling is coyned.

If the Moon be in conjunction or aspect with any Planet, and neither of them have latitude, the Crisis will be firm; if they differ much in latitude, the Crisis will be weak. The Moon in conjunction with SATURN at the decumbiture shews long sickness; and if SATURN be slow in motion, so much the worse (and bad is the best) at all times in such a case.

If Saturn be retrograde when he comes to the opposition of the Sun, beware of a relapse.
If SATURN have North latitude, be sure the sock is bound much in body. If the Moon be joyned to a retrograde Planet, the sick vomits up his Physick.

VENUS helpes more in the Sicknesses of young men and women, then she doth in old.

If the disease come of heat, VENUS helps more than JUPITER; if the disease comes more of cold, JUPITER helps more than VENUS. If the disease comes of Love, there is not a more pestilent Planet in the Heavens then VENUS; then call for help of JUPITER; in persecutions of Religion, JUPITER is little better then the Divel; call help of VENUS in such a case.

MERCURY occidental and strong, signifies good in diseases.

IF MARS cause the disease, VENUS helps more then JUPITER; If SATURN, then JUPITER more then VENUS.

If in the beginning or a sickness the moon be in conjuction with any fixed Stars of the first magnitude, whose latitude from the Ecliptick is but small, you may safely judge of diseases by the nature of that Star she is joyned to: suppose he be of the nature of a Planet good or bad, take him according to his nature.

When the Moon is joyned to any planet by body or aspect in the beginning of any Sickness, if she aspect that Planet when she comes to the quartile or opposition of the place, the Crisis will be firm and stable, and 'twill move no faster then a house, and 'twill not be altered be it good or bad.

But if when she comes to the quartile or opposition, she meets with another Planet, be sure the disease changes either to better or worse, according to that star she meets withall.
And this will appear in the sick party, or else in the Physitian, or in the course of Physick.

See what house the Planet she meets withall at the Crisis is Lord of in the decumbiture, and judge accordingly; and so a sick person may happen to have more wit then an old doting Physitian.

If it be a fixed star of another nature to that fixed star she was withall at the decumbiture, it will not alter so much, or at least there will not be a universal alteration of the disease; and my reason is, because the fixed stars are so far from the Earth. And the last thing is,

Whatsoever is said of the Moon in acute diseases, will hold as true of the Sun in Chronick Diseases.

+ + + + + + + + +

LIB. 11

ASTROLOGICAL JUDGEMENT UPON DISEASES
OR

A Methodical way to find out the Cause, Nature, Symptoms, and change of a Disease, together with the parts of the afflicted, the exact time of recovery, or dissolutions by the Decumbiture; Amplified by Examples.

The Basis of the Story was borrowed from BOEL DURST Cosmographer to the King of FRANCE, and the most excellent Cardinal the Duke of RICHELIEU.

'Tis confest, in some place I have abbreviated him, in others corrected him; let another doe the like by me; What I have done, I have done, and am not ashamed the world should see it. Through the never failing mercies of God, I had an opportunity put into my hand to finish this so much desired, so long wished for work; if there be any weaknesse in it, it is my own; if there be any excellency in it, give God the glory.

He that writes Ignominy upon the backside of another man's book, never setting forth any of his own, let the name of Ignominy be branded, and not ingraven upon his Sepulchre.

I would fain see the piss Prophets of this age deliver such a judgement of diseases by the Urine; he that can do so, ERIT MIHI MAGNUS APOLLO. Why do I trouble my head with the Physitians, whose Covetousness or Lazinesse, or both, or something worse, will not suffer them to study those Arts which are essentially to their Monopolized calling; but I will be silent, for their fall is approaching by reason of their pride, if he wrote true that writes, that pride goes before a fall, and a haughty mind before destruction: my Genius is too dull to comprehend my Author, or to give him the thousandth part of his due praise. I desire to be censured by Dr. EXPERIENCE, who will give judgement without partiality; and I hope 'tis no disparagement to MONSIEUR DURST that I deliver him in my own language.

Chap 1
The Definitions of the Word Crisis, its Use, Cause, Kinds, Division and Difference.

Crisis according to Gallon, is a swift and suddain change of any disease, whereby the sick is either brought to recovery, or death and a sick man can be brought to nothing else, unless you will make him a beast of a man. For every swift and suddain change wherever it happens, whether in the Moon or in the Air, or sick body, GALEN plays the man and calls a Crisis, and from this Crisis judgement given, whether the sick be likely to live or die.

The word Crisis is derived from a Greek word which signifieth to judge or discern, or pass sentence upon a thing; therefore Critical dayes are nothing else but dayes wherein a man may discern a disease, or give judgement upon it, be it good or bad, it matters not much, 'tis taken by a Metaphor from the judicial Court to the Art of Physick, because, 'tis something like to plead a man's cause for his life, and to labour acutely under a disease to be drawn by inimical accusers before the judgement Seat, and to run the hazard of life, with a cruel and hostil Disease. Moreover there are three things requisite to a judicial Court, the Accuser, the Person indicted, and the Judge. So likewise are there three things by which the Art of Physick consisteth, and by which every cure is perfected. 1. The Disease. 2. Nature, and the Physitian, which is nature's servant, or at least should be so: and 3. the accidents which manifest what the disease is, and stand as witnesses.

The cause of the Crisis is twofold, inward and outward, the internal cause is taken from its own proper principle, if you will believe HIPPOCRATES, and that is double or twofold; for either nature labours to expell the tumour that causeth the disease, or else the humour it self being drawn to a place, and not fit for Excretion, by its own weight or quality, burdens nature, and so break out. HIPPOCRATES was but a man, and I am no more; a man saith he, is troubled when he is in feaver, and the sign is horror, tremblings, running hither, and thither throughout the Microcosm, this is one internal cause.

THE SECOND INTERNAL CAUSE:

Others: there be, `tis no matter who, that ascribe the efficient cause of the Crisis to nature itself; Nature if she be strong, is a good Physitian for all diseases, and separates that which is good from that which is bad, and having done so, prepares that which breeds annoyances for Excretion, and at last makes a shift to cast it out.

The external cause of the Crisis, is caused by an alteration of the Aire, whence ariseth an alteration of the breath a man draws in, from cold to hear, from dry to moist, or the contraries to them both.

For HIPPOCRATES himself in his sixth Aphorism and in his Treatise DE NATURA HUMANA speaks in down dunstable language, that heat and moisture in the body, moves forward the Crisis: for diseases, some saith he, come by ill Dyet, other by the Aire we draw in.

So then the Dyet as it breeds such humours in the body, is internal, but the Air we draw in, is the external cause of the Crisis.

And now give me leave to leave my Author, and yet I will not forget him quite either. The Lord eternal in the beginnings when he made the Creation, made it of a composition of contraries; discord makes a harmony as in musicke, if the world be composed of a composition of contraries, various must needs be the disposition of man's life: Whence comes sometimes health, sometimes sicknesse, sometimes melancholy, sometimes choler to the body of man, and happy is that man that knows himself:

These qualities in man altered by the various influences of the Stars, the Sphere of the one carrying a swifter motion then the sphere of the other, then various must needs be the disposition of man's body.
The Luminaries carry the greatest strength in the heavens,and so do the time servers in the State, and this needs not be doubtful to any body, if you consider that the sound of a Drum or Trumpet incites a man to valour, and the sound of a Fiddle to dancing. Besides, other manifest effects of the Luminaries appeare to our eyes. Who makes hours and dayes, and seasons in the year ? is it not the Sun who makes alterations in the Aire, in Plants, and in living Creatures? what is the reason that Oysters are fuller at the full Moon, then at the new ? To the number of Oysters, joine Crabs and Lobsters, nay the marrow in the body of Man; is it not the Moon ? A man if he pleaseth may say his

right hand is his left, and a prating Priest may preach his pleasure; let Doctor Experience be judge. Now then we have brought the matter to this purpose, that the universal cause of the Crisis is the influence of the Heavens: for the Celestial bodies, either by heat, light, motion, or aspects, configuration, or all of them, or some of them, act not only in the four Elements, but Elementary bodies; for if they act in the one they must needs in the other, and then by consequences in man, which is but compounded by Elements.

The Earth is a great lump of dirt rolled up together, and by an only wise God hanged in the Air: the Stars are no more, neither is the Moon; only what mettle the Sun is.made of I know not'

But if the bodies of men are elementary, composed of Fire, Aire, Earth, and Water, he must needs participate in one measure or other, of all these Elements. The Elements being contraries, cannot always agree; hence comes the cause of health, sometimes of sickness, sometimes death it self; and ARISTOTLE was half of my opinion when he wrote these words: From the rain and dew of Heaven both good and bad things are caused to bud.

KINDS OF CRISIS

The kinds of Crisis are two; one is acute diseases; and they are to be judged by the Moon; the other in long and lasting, or chronick diseases, which are to be judged of by the Sun; For those Crises which come from their own proper principle are from th internal cause depending only upon the motions of the Moon, and her Configurations and aspects to the place she was in at the Decumbiture.

If you must note in your acute diseases the aspects or radiations of the Moon, to wit, her Quartile or Opposition, are not taken from the Conjunction of the Moon to the Sun, as they are in Almanacks or Ephemerides, which is but the Father of the Almanack, but from the place in which the Moon was found at the Decumbiture, as shall appear by a few examples hereafter.

There are Acute and Chronick diseases.

Of Acute Diseases, some are simply acute, others are peracute, others are very acute, per-per-acute, or exceeding acute.

Those which are simply acute, are finished in 8, 10, 11, 14, 20, 21, dayes, and they are called monthly diseases by some, and lunary by others, and they none of the greatest fools neither: they are terminated in the time the Moon traceth the 12 Celestial Signs of the Zodiack, which is in. 27 dayes, some odd hours, and some odd minutes.

These acute diseases which suffer changes, or degenerate, are to be judged by an imperfect way; for sometimes they increase, sometimes they are remitted; they are as fickle as a weather cock,: according as the Moon meets with the beams either of good or evil Planets: and that is not all the trick they have neither; For sometimes they change out of Acute diseases into Chronick diseases; and so a continual Fever may change into a Hectick Fever; or an intermitting Fever into a continual Fever; and this disease terminates in forty days; very acute diseases, such as are concluded in 5, 6, 7, or 8, days, among which is an inflammation of the Lungs.

Exceeding acute diseases, they are such which end in three or four dayes at furthest, as Pestilences, Apoplexies, &c.

Chronick diseases follow the motion of the Sun, and 'tis about ninety days before the first Crisis appears, for in that time the Sun comes to the comes to the proper quartile of the place he was in at Decumbiture, as appears in Hecktick Fevers, Dropsies: but when he comes to his Sextile, or Trine Aspect of the place he was in at the Decumbiture, some motion appears whereby a man if he have any guts in his brains, may judge of the Crisis to come. It falls out well, if the Sun be well aspected by good Planets; and worse if to evil Planets: and this holds true, if you consider it from the Nativity, throughout all the whole course of a man's life, if Doctor Experience tell truth. Moreover of the Crises, some are perfect, some are imperfect.

A perfect Crisis is when the disease appears intirely, and perfectly to be judged of; and this is sometimes hopefull, when there is great probability of health and recovery; desperate, when there is palpable signs of death. An imperfect Crisis, is when the disease is changed upon every light occasion; and if MARS be the Author of the disease, and in a signe of a double body, upon my life you shall not fail; for the Crisis happens as true as the Weather-cock.

Your fastest way then is to judge of the disease, is by the Aspects of the Moon to the Planets: when the Moon meets with the inimical or hostile beams of SATURN or MARS, have a care of your Patient: And if you know what hinders, by the same reason you may know what helps. Physitians in former times, when they were wise, and minded the common good, and not their own gain, they distinguished the Crisis of the diseases thus:

Some were safe, some doubtful: some fit to be judged, and some not fit to be judged.

That Crisis is safe which comes without great and pernicious aspects.

It is doubtful, suspicious, and I had almost said dangerous, which comes with great pernicious aspects.

The disease is fit to be judged, when signs of concoction come the fourth day, and then certainly the Crisis will appear the ninth. The Moon moves not upon an equal motion; therefore you had best trust to her motion rather than the dayes.

The Sun hath dominion in Chronick diseases, the Moon in acute; if you be a wise man, your judgement shall be as sure as the Sun, and that never fails without a miracle.

In times of yore, when knowledge was scant, men went a begging for it; and they that had gotten knowledge, monopolized it. A few glimpses of ADAM'S happiness in Paradise, which happiness all the world have been reaching after ever since.

They knew well enough the Moon moved so many degrees in so many days: an evil Angel (I had almost said the Devil) perceiving there was want of knowledge in the world, goes and transforms himself into an Angel of light, and taught men to count the time by dayes: 'Tis no great marvel the AEGYPTIANS would worship Garlic and Onyons for Gods, when we deifie CHRISTMAS-DAY, though perhaps it may be cloudy.

What I have spoken, I have only spoken to show that it is the motion of the Sun & Moon that produceth the Crisis in diseases, and not the days.

I must return to the place I intended; Of days some are called by their own name, Critical days; others are called Judicial days, and they are so called, because upon them dame Nature and her son Dr. Reason, would make manifest what the disease is, and Dr. Experience tells me 'tis true. Another time is called Intercidental, which is a time falls out between the Judicial days and Critical. Upon these Intercidental days the disease is usually remitted; if so, then a good Crisis may be expected; if not, an evil. I shall explain these terms before I go further, a man falls sick, there is the first Crisis, let the cause of the disease be what you will; when the Moon comes to the same degree of the next sign she was in at the Decumbiture, there is the Judicial day; for in that time the disease shews it self in its colours, with bag and baggage. When the Moon comes to her Sextile, it brings the Intercidental day, and should mitigate the disease; if she do not, she is aspected to evil Planets: and if she be aspected to ill Plants, an ill Crisis is to be expected, and so the contrary; and you shall never find this fail.

CHAPTER II.
The way to finde out the Critical dayes, as also the Decumbiture, both by Ancient and Modern Writers.

Ancient Physitians, because they were ignorant of the motion of the Moon, though not of her operation, as many of our modern are, made their account by number of dayes; and in so doing, erred egregiously; And although DURET my Author quotes their opinions, I hold it not worth time to recite men's failings. But of the certain term or time when the Critical days begin, I shall quote these few words.

When any notable disease comes, if you would discern whether it tends to Health, Death, Mutation, or Continuance, it is necessary that you begin at the first punct of time of invasion of the disease This GALEN saith is very hard, if not impossible to find; 'tis taken PRO CONFESSO, that it may be easily known, when a man takes his bed in his sickness; but when the beginning of the sickness is, that's the question: For a lusty Stout man bears the disease longer, and is longer before he takes his bed, then a puny weak sickly man is: a meer suspition of a Sicknesse will send a fainthearted man to bed; you may perswade him he is sick, whether he be or no.

Notwithstanding this is most certain, that in most acute diseases, as also in many other diseases, as the Falling Sicknesse, Palsies, Apoplexies, Pluresies, &c. 'tis an easy thing to find out the beginning, or the precise time of the invasion of the disease.

The common opinion of such as are learned in Astrology is, and according to their opinion I affirme, that the moment of time is to be taken for the beginning of the disease, in which a man finds a manifest pain or hurt in his body: for instance, when a man hath got a fever, usually the head akes certain days before; this is not the Fever, but a Messenger or forerunner of the Fever; the true beginning of the Fever is when the disease appeares sensibly, or when a horrour or trembling invades the Sick, as does usually in the beginning of a Fever: that is the beginning of the disease, when the disease appears manifest to sense; and this was the judgement of HIPPOCRATES, one of the honestest of

Physitians: And you shall find this always, that the more
acute the disease is, the more manifest the beginning of it is
to sense: yea, so manifest, that it is almost impossible that
the beginning should lie hid from any one that wants
reason, if he have but sense.

CHAPTER III.
Of the Sympathy and Antipathy of the Signes and Planets.

Before we come to Prognostick, we must know that there is
a Sympathy between Celestial and Terrestrial bodies; which
will easily appear, if we consider that the whole creation is
one entire and united body, composed by the power of an
All-wise God, of a composition of discords.

Also there is friendship and hatred between one
sign of the Zodiack and another; for fiery signs are contrary
to watry, and nocturnal to diurnal, &c.

The Planets are also friendly and inimical one to
another; but in their friendship and enmity, whatever the
matter it, I cannot agree with neither ancient nor modern
Writers. And when I cannot do so, I fly to Dr. Reason for
advise; they hold MARS and VENUS to be friends. And
what your opinion is of all the rest, you may find by Mr.
LILLIES Introduction; My own opinion grounded upon
reason, is this, that there are two causes of friendship and
enmity between Planets. Essential and Accidental: Planets
are essentially inimical three ways.

First, when their Houses or Exaltations are opposite
one to the others; and so SATURN is an enemy to both
Luminaries, JUPITER to MERCURY, MARS to VENUS.

2. Planets are inimical one to the other, when their
temperatures or qualities are opposites; and so JUPITER is
an enemy to SATURN, he being hot and moist, SATURN
cold and dry: So MARS is enemy to VENUS, he being hot
and dry, she cold and moist.

3. Planets are inimical when their conditions differ;
so there is enmity between Sol and Saturn for one loves the

Court, and the other the Country; JUPITER is enemy to
MARS for he loves peace and justice, MARS violence and
oppressions; MARS is enemy to VENUS, for he rejoyceth in
the field, she in the bed; he loves to be public, she plays least
in sight. And thus you see in every respect, what a difficult
thing it is to make MARS and VENUS rationally friends.

Accidental inimicalness to Planets, is when they are
in square or opposition, &c. the one to the other. Also
Inimicalness must needs be in the Signs; for if cold and heat,
moisture and dryness be inconsistent together in one and
the same place, as your eyes will tell you, if you will but
please to take a pail of water & throw it into the fire, then
can they not be in one and the same place in the heavens.
And if so, as is most true, then myst signs be, some cold,
some hot, and some moist; and seeing the first qualities are
adverse the one to the other, there is necessity, that
sometimes one must yield, and sometimes overcome: and
this is the reason of the corruption, generation, and
vicissitude of things.
Moreover, the Moon constituted in a Sign, commonly
strikes upon the nature of the sign she is in: as if she be in a
fiery sign, she stirs up Choler, &c.

Also as every Element hath two qualities, so hath
every celestial sign; the Aerial signs are hot and moist, the
Earthly signs cold and dry; the Fiery signs hot and dry, the
Watery signs cold and moist; For Aery signs are joyned to
fiery by heat, and to watry by moisture, and to earthly by
coldness; the Earthly are joyned to the watry by coldness,
and to fiery by dryness: this is an old true maxim of
Philosophers, which I shall not at this time be captious
against.

Besides, the congress and the configurature of the
Planets and fixed Stars is diligently to be heeded; of these
some are obnoxious and hatefull; a Quartile and
Opposition, as also the Conjunction of bad Planets; others
are healthful, as Sextile and Trine, and Conjunction of good
Planets; and indeed the chiefest part of Astrology consisteth

in the due observation of configurations; for by these some alterations in things below, either to better or worse, according to the nature of the Planets or Stars are jouyned with, or aspected to one another, they seminate something in Sub-Lunary bodies according to their own nature: If dissention be between the stars, the sperm proves malicious and destructive, and tumultuous; even as the opposition of winds, especially the North and South winds, produceth thunder, lightning, and pestilential vapours; and this we find never fails if the South-wind prevails, and the Moon and MERCURY behold one another.

Thus you see a reason, if you know but what a reason is, or ever heard of such a thing, why diseases in the body of a man are either exasperated, or remitted, according to the good or evil meeting of the Planets.

Of the Aspects, Opposition is the worst of all by any contrariety or diversity of nature of the Signs in which the Oppositions fall out; but in respect of the Planets themselves opposing, which beong at the greatest distance are most inimical they being in a posture to outface one another, and this is the most principal cause of enmity.

A Quartile is inimical, because the Stars so aspected be in signs of contrary nature; as SOL in ARIES, LUNA in CANCER, the aspect is hateful, because ARIES is hot and dry, CANCER cold and moist; ARIES masculine, CANCER feminine; ARIES diurnal, CANCER nocturnal.

And now by the leave of my Author, and also the great PTOLEMY himself, and of all the sons of art this day living, who build their judgement on Dr. TRADITION, and not upon the sound principles of Dr. REASON, if this be the Original of the enmity of a square aspect, as is agreed upon all sides.

Then, why do they hold that a Quartile in Signes of long ascentions is aequivalent to a Trine, and a Trine in Signs of short ascentions as pernicious as a Square ? put the rest of the non-sence into the bundel, and when you have done, look upon it a little while; and when you have viewed it a little, tell be I pray; Doth the longness or shortness of the ascentions adde or take away any thing from the quality of the Signs ?

Is not this the way, the onely way to bring the Art into a Labyrinth, if not into a confusion? In truth, in my opinion it is. This I will confess, and give you my reason for it when I have done; one Square is not so bad as another; as from ARIES to CANCER, is worse than from CANCER to LIBRA, because the Signs CANCER and LIBRA are in better harmony, as agreeing in passive qualities, namely, moisture; whereas ARIES and CANCER disagree totally. By this rule you may find out the rest.

Also this I affirm, and will prove it when I have done, that some Semisextiles are worse than some Quartiles; for PISCES is more inimical to ARIES then to CAPRICORNE; first because it is the twelfth Sign from him: 2. besides disagrees more in qualities.

A Sextile Aspect is good, because the Signs which are in Sextile the one to the other, are both of the same active quality, both of a sex, both of a time; for example, Aries and Gemini are both masculine, Diurnal; Taurus and Cancer are both cold, both Feminine, both Nocturnal; but because they differ all in passive qualities, it, is not altogether so friendly as Trine aspect is; for that consists altogether of Signs of the same nature, sex, quality, and time, and are correspondent the one to the other every way. A Conjunction or Synod is the strongest of all, and cannot properly be called an aspect. A Conjunction of good Planets with good, is exceeding good, it is good in the highest degree; a Conjunction of bad Planet's with bad Planets is as bad, as the former was good; a Conjunction of good Planets with bad, is no ways commendable. I have now done, if you will be pleased but to take notice, that the conjunction of all Planets with the Sun is bad, because the Sun, who gives them their efficacy, takes it away at such times. I would be Critical at this, but I shall forbear at this time.

Liber II

Chapter IV

The way of finding out the Critical and Judicial dayes by a Figure of eight hours.

      This is the method of HIPPOCRATES, and from him GALEN used, and it is to be done in this manner.

1. Make your Scheme of eight equal parts.
2. Search out the Sign, Degree, and Minute the Moon was in at the beginning of the sickness.
3. Place the sign, degree, and minute the Moon was in at the beginning of the sickness upon the cusp of the first house, as though that were ascending at the time.
4. Add forty five degrees to this; you need not regard the,latitude of the Region, for it is of no use in Critical Figures; but take the degrees barely from the Eckliptick, when you have added forty five degrees to the place of the Moon at the decumbiture; the point of the Zodiack answerable to that shall make the cusps of the second house.
5. Forty five degrees more added to that, will bring you to the Cuspe of the third House, to which when the Moon comes, she comes to the Quartile of the place she was in at the decumbiture; and this makes the first Crisis.
6. Forty five degrees more added to this, makes the fourth house; 45 degrees more added to that points out the place of the true opposition of the Moon to the place she was in at the Decumbiture; and this makes the second Crisis. The second Quartile of the Moon to her own place at the decumbiture, makes the third Crisis. And the fourth is when she comes to the same sign, degree, and minute, that she was in at the decumbiture.

      The time or houses noted betwixt the Crisis, are called the judicial times, or such times wherein a man may judge what the disease is, or what it will be; remember this all along in such kinds of judgment; and do not forget not to number the time by dayes, as the ancients did; for they were, either ignorant, or regardlesse of the course of the Moon; for the Moon comes to the Judicial or Critical days sometimes sooner, sometimes later, as she is either swifter or slower in motion.

Now the time called Critical, is always evil, because of the contrareity of the sign the Moon is in when to the sign she was in before, or the contrareity of her nature to the opposite place: at such a time there ariseth a controversie or battell, as it were between the disease and nature; the Moon maintains nature in acute diseases: And now you have the reason why, that if she be afflicted upon a Critical day by the bodies, or ill beams of SATURN and MARS, or the Lord of death, (which is always Lord of the eighth house, and sometimes Lord of the fourth House, will serve the turn, if he be malevolent, because he signifies the grave,) the disease increaseth, and sometime the sick dies: But if the Moon at the time of the Crisis beholds the Lord of the Ascendant, or the fortunatecs fortunately health ensues; for the malady is vanquished and routed in the conflict.

If the disease terminate upon the first Crisis, see how the Moon is configured on the second Crisis, and judge then by the same rules.

If it terminate not then neither, as sometimes such a thing happens, view the third Crisis, and judge by that same way; if your judgement balanced by reason, and the former rules, certifie you the disease will not end one way nor other, neither in health nor death; see what you can say to the Moon when she returns to the place she was in at the Decumbiture, which is about twenty seven days, eight hours, and some minutes; and see how the Moon is then seated, and to what Planets she is configurated then; and this of necessity must be the end of all acute diseases.

Thus you see an acute disease can last but a moneth at longest; not one in a hundred lasteth so long; not one in twenty lasteth above half so long.

If the disease end not then, the acute disease is turned into a Chronick disease; and all Chronick diseases must be judged by the Sun. The rules of judging of

Chronical diseases by the Sun, are the same by which we judge the acute diseases by the Moon.

As for Judicial days, (I suppose he means the Intercidental time which fall out between the first and judicial dayes in Crisis) which fall out just in the midst betwixt the Critical days, I shall passe them by at this time, because I fancy not this way of judgment by a Figure of eight houses; yet I shall not passe them by, but that I shall remember them in this Treatise.

Chapter V
The former rules illustrated by an Example.

A Certain man fell sick of an Acute disease at PARIS in FRANCE, Anno 1641. Jan 12, about eight of the clock in the afternoon, at which time the Moon was posited in AQUARIUS, 10° 19'. This I place in the Ascendant.

To this AQUARIUS 10° 19' I adde 45 degrees; the product in PISCES 25° 19' which makes the first Judicial time.

To which adding 45 degrees more, it will bring you to TAURUS 10° 19' to which place when the Moon arrives, she comes to the exact quartile of the place she was in at the decumbiture, and makes the first Crisis.

Adde 45 degrees to that, and it produceth GEMINI 25° 19' which is the second judicial time.

If you would know when the second Crisis comes about, it is but only adding 45 degrees to that, and you will find the result to be LEO 10° 19' just the place opposit to the Moon at the decumbiture. The remainder is found out in the same manner.

When you have done so, it is not more but this. First, Seek the time when the Moon comes to TAURUS 10° 19' and you shall find it comes upon the 19th of JAN' about eight of the Clock at night.

Secondly, View first the face of heaven, Secondly the position and configuration of the Planets one with the

another at the same time. VIDE GEORGE WHARTON
HEMEROSCOPEION 1652, his Discourse at large.
(See Table)

The History of this observation is of a certaine
person, who by reason of great wear inesse in a journey,
was supprised with a Fever at the time before mentioned;
together with his Fever he had a Cough and a Plurisie.

The original of this disease is Choler putrefied with
blood in the veines, and is the most viilent of all Fevers. The
night after the decumbiture the Fever appear'd, although on
the third day all shaking left him, yet felt not the Patient the
least intermission, the Moon being in AQUARIUS 10° 19"
AQUARIUS being also a signe of infirmity, the Moon being
in Sextile to MARS applying to VENUS and SATURNE,
MARS afflicting the Sun with a Quartile, as also JUPITER
and MERCURY who were in combustion.

The 16th day of the same moneth of JANUARY the
disease increased, at which time the Moon came to a
Semi-quadrant making the first judicial time. And meeting
then with never an Aspect, the Crisis could be expected no
other then doubtful and unfortunate.

The 19th day of the same moneth at eight of the
clock in the afternoon, the first Crisis came about, some little
sweat the diseased had. And if I may be bold to leave my
Author for a little time, if you view the presages of
HIPPOCRATES, which you shall find at the latter end of
this book:
The words run thus, or to this purpose: It is very hopeful
when a man sick of a Fever sweats upon a Critical day;
however my Author confesses, that both his Cough, and his
paine in his side left him, though his Fever still remained,
nay increased, by reason of the Quartile of MARS and
VENUS at the same time, MERCURY being Lord of the
Ascendant at the Decumbiture. Also it is worth noting, that
the Moon being in AQUARIUS at the Decumbiture, and
comes to TAURUS at the first Crisis, both TAURUS and
AQUARIUS are of infirmity; yet you see the Plurisie left

him, the Moone being strong in her exaltation, though void of course.

CRITICAL DATES		MOON'S MOTION		TIME OF INCIDENCE		Lunar state, according to the Decumbiture, her aspects, also the mutual aspects of aspecting Planets.
		January 12th		DAY	Hour Min ute	Moon to sextile MARS to VENUS & SATURN.
Decumbiture						conjunction SUN JUPITER MERCURY SQUARE SUN MARS
		10°	AQUARIUS 19'	12th	8h 00 p.m.	Moon VACUA, no good Crisis to be expected
Judicat. 1		25°	PISCES 19'	16th	5h 43 a.m.	
1.	Crisis	10°	TAURUS 19'	19th	8h 00 p.m.	square MARS; VENUS: VACUA
2	Judicial	25°	GEMINI 19'	23rd	2h 36 p.m.	Moon to trine SATURN. Threatens an ill Crisis
2.	Crisis	10°	LEO 19'	27th	5h 50 a.m.	Moon VACUA, an ill Crisis.
3.	Judicial	25°	VIRGO 19'	30th	3h 44 p.m.	Moon to trine SATURN JUPITER A good crisis to be hoped
3.	Crisis	10°	SCORPIO 19'	February 2nd	9h 01 p.m.	Moon to trine VENUS, he recovers.
4.	Judicial	25°	SAGITTARIUS 19			
4.	Crisis	10°	AQUARIUS 19'			

Table 1

I pass by my Authors infirmities in this and other things.

JANUARY 23. When the Moon by transit made the second judicial time, she was afflicted by the trine of SATURNE, which prognosticates cause enough of fear in the second Crisis.

JANUARY 27. at 5h 50 in the morning, the Moon came to the true opposition, to the place she was in at the Decumbiture, she being then without any Aspect, either good or evil; this brought no hopes of cure to the sick man at that time; and indeed the sick was at that time very bad;

yea, so bad that his Physitians were in doubt whether he would live or die.

JANUARY 30. at 3 hours 44 minutes after noon, comes about the third judicial time, at which time the Moon was in Trine to JUPITER, which gives strong hopes that a healthful and propitious Crisis would ensue, and so it did; for upon

FEBRUARY the second, at nine a clock after noon, the Moon coming to 10 degrees 9 minutes of the Scorpion, where she made the second Quartile to the place she was in at the decumbiture; and the third Crisis she applyed to the trine of beautiful VENUS, his Fever began to leave him, and he began to attain his pristine health.

By this one example you may see the wonderful harmony and consent of diseases with the motions of the Heavens, which that it may appear more clear, and be visible to all, unless it be to such are so blind they will not see; myAuthor adjoyns a rational Figure of the decumbiture, and gives his judgement upon it.

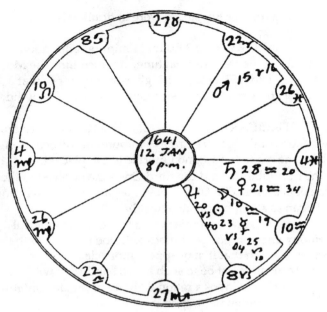

The Chief Significations of this Figure are the Ascendant
and Mercury Lord of it, Retrograde in Capricorne, a
moveable Signe in the 5th House of the Heaven, and in the
House of Saturne.

The 6th house and his Lord Saturn in Aquarius, in the 6th
House strong and potent.

The Moon in the 6th house upon the cuspe of it; Sol in the
5th House with the Lord of the eighth afflicted by the
Quartile of Mars in a fiery Signe; this plainly shewes a
disease of Choler.

Jupiter in a moveable Sign in the 5th House,
who rules the Stomack, Liver and Sides, combust
and in Quartile to Mars, stirred up a Pleurisie,
and Mercury afflicted shewed a dry Cough. Hence
it appears that Monsieur DURET was no Physitian;

for if he had, he would easily have known that a Plrisie never comes without a dry Cough; the most excellent of men may have failings.

The Moon in Aquarius appling to Saturn at the beginning of the disease, shewes the disease comes of weariness, according to the Doctrine both of HIPPOCRATES and HERMES; but here arises another question; Shall the disease be long or short ? This is answered thus: the fixed Signe upon the cuspe of the 6th House shewes length of the disease.

Saturn in the 6th House shews no less, but tells the same tale.

Again Saturn Lord of the 6th stronger then the Lord of the Ascendant, shewes a violent increase of the disease. Seeing Mars in a fiery signe afflicts both Luminaries, the Sun by a Quartile, and the Moon by a Sextile; hence we may safely gather, that Saturn and Mars are Authors of the disease, and two part stakes between them; the one made it violent, the other continuing.

Give me leave not a little to passe my judgment upon this Figure; when first I viewed the Figure, upon the first blush I admired the man would live, the Lord of the Ascendant being combust, and applyed to the Sun, Mars casting Antiscion to the Sun, the Moon upon the cusp of the 6th CUM MULTIS ALIIS; The onely reasons that I could finde of the life, were these:

1. Saturne and Mars are both strong, and neither of them Lord of death, though both of them skew themselves like potent enemies, that are able to hurt their foe, but scorn it; though they are enemies to life, yet they are honourable enemies, because strong.

2. The Moon applyes not immediately to Saturne, but to the body of Mercury, who is Lord of the 10th which shews the disease might be cured by Physick if a wise Physitian had it in hand.

3. There is a Reception between the Sun and Mars which tyes the sword of Mars from killing.

4. Venus beautifieth the signification of the 6th house,almost as much as Saturne deforms it.

5. Neither Saturne nor Mars behold the Ascendant, and thats good.

6. The disease came by the mans own misguiding himself, because the Lord of the 12th and Ascendant are together.

7. The Moon applies to a fortune which hath triplicity in the Ascendant, though in an ill House.

8. I am confident the man journeyed again so soon as he was well; First, because Mars Lord of the end, is near the House of journeys at the decumbiture; Secondly, because the Moon applyes to the Lady of the third House at the decumbiture, which is Venus.

Chapter VI.
The way to set a Figure of 16 Houses.

The way of setting this Figure, differs nothing from the former, save onely that the Heavens are divided into twice as many parts. The manner of erecting it, is this, the true place of the Moon being taken at the decumbiture, place that upon the cusp of the Ascendant, as though it were Ascending at the time, to which adde 22 degrees 30 minutes and you have the first intercidental time, 22°30' being added to that skew the second intercidental time, and as many added to them bring about the first Crisis; this shall be clearly skewed in this Example. A Figure of Crisis in 16. [See Table 2]

The History of this second observation is of a certain religious person, some monke or Fryer a hundred to one else; who is 1640, December the ninth, STILO NOVO, was taken with a feaver and shivering at eight o'clock in the morning, the next day the shivering left him, the Feaver remaining, the Feaver seeming like a Hemitritaer, or double tertian, or a Causos, which is a continual burning Feaver; which of them soever it was, this is certain, it arose from some Cholerick matter.

CRITICAL DATES	MOON'S MOTION	TIME OF INCIDENCE		State and Aspects of the Moon and other Planets.
Decumbiture	27 Libra 18	9th	8hr00am	Moon to Trine Saturn; Saturn to Mercury, Venus, Jupiter
1 Interc.	19 Scorpio 48	10th	8h40pm	to square Saturn 6 trine Mars
1st Judic.	12 sagitarius 18	12th	21h12pm	
2nd Interc.	4 Capricorne 48	13th	10h13pm	conjunct Jupiter, Venus
1st Crisis	27 Capricorne 18	15th	a little pm	Sextile Moon and Mars, an ill crisis
3rd Interc.	19 Aquarius 48	17th	2h00am	Sextile Sun and Saturn
2nd Judic.	12 Pisces 18	18th		Moon applies to Mercury, Venus and Jupiter arguing a hopeful Crisis at which he recovered

Table 2

The second day it had another accesse, and the third a worse then that.

The place of the Moon at the decumbiture was in a preterited trine of Saturne. The Moon applied to the Sextile of Mercury, Venus, and Jupiter.

The Fifteenth day of the same moneth of December appears the first Crisis; and though to sweat well many medicines were applyed, and those powerful; yet the Feaver gave not way an inch, because the Moon applyed to Mars, and the Sun to Saturne, though by good aspects, neither was it mitigated till the eighteenth day, at which time the Moon applyed to Mercury, Venus and Jupiter.

Here was that Aphorism of HIPPOCRATES ratified, Chap. 5. Aphorism 15 that if the Moon be not afflicted at the decumbiture, yet if she be with the beams of the Malevolents at the Crisis, a good Crisis is not to be expected, but health will be staved off.

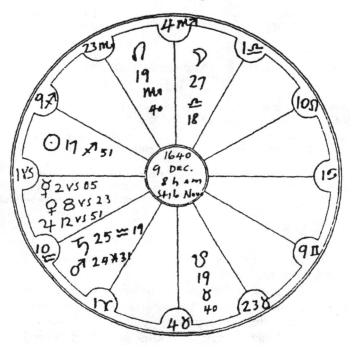

An Astrological Judgment upon the Figure.

    I Confesse in this judgement my Author is very faulty; he is dead, and I shall not make known his faults: however this is true; In this figure Capricorn is upon the cuspe of the ascendent; and it is a moveable figure, therefore the disease is likely to be short.

    2. Saturn Lord of it, is very potent and strong in his own house, and swift in course; there's a second Argument.

    3. Both fortunes in the ascendent may well make up a third.

    4. The Moon applying to the fortunes, makes up a fourth; this is enough; only the Quartile of the Sun and Mars showes the sickness of Choler.

I could give you mine own observations upon this disease, if I would; but let it alone and leave every man to his own heuretes.

Chapter VII.
How to set a Figure of twelve Houses for the Crisis.

This seems to be the most rational of all the rest; and it is the most easily and readily done; and it may be that's the reason my Author left it out, though he promised it. And indeed the wayes of God are all easy, very easy, 'Tis the wayes of men that are crabbed and difficult.

I shall first of all shew you the way how to do it; secondly give you an Example of mine own upon it.

First of all if you would know how to make such a critical Figure upon a decumbiture, make you a Figure after the vulgar form; then note when what signe, degree and minute of the Moon is in at the decumbiture; set that signe, degree and minute on the ascendent, and thirty degrees to that, and the same degree and minute of the next sign will be upon the Cusp of the second house; the work is as easie as walking up and down without a staff, as I shall by and by make appear by an example.

Then be pleased to take notice, that the first house is the decumbiture, the second the judiciak time, the third the intercidental; which word Dr. PHAGE of NIDHURST in SUSSEX, in his book called SPECULUM AEGROTORUM, so sillily translates MORTALL, mistaking the word CAEDO to kill, for CADEO to fall: wherein the man most egregiously shewed his deficiency, both in Schollership and Physick: yet this commendation I'le give him, his heart was more free to do good, then his brain was able.

The fourth house brings the first Crisis about: and when you come to that, begin again as you did before: you may see the way without a pair of spectacles by the decumbiture that I have quoted: you may take it PRO CONFESSO, if you please, that I have many Decumbitures by me. But I want time to insert them; or if I did not, I would not blot paper with them.

Be pleased to accept this one, in lieu of all the rest.

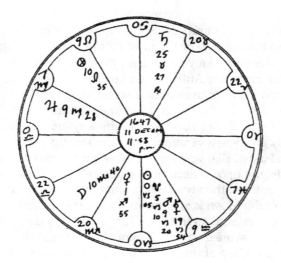

This unhappy creature being untowardly matched with an unnatural husband, came up to London and lived in a service; and in her service was surprised with a furious disease at the time, and under the face of heaven before noted.

I shall first give a rational judgement of the Figure, and afterwards treat of the Crisis.

The person of this young woman is signified by Venus in Sagittarius; and truly, I believe she was an upright dealing creature. That the cause of her disease lay hid, or at least very obscure is plainly signified by so many Planets being under the earth.

That she procured her own disease, because the Lord of the 6th is in the twelfth; As also because the Lord of the Ascendant is disposed by a Planet in the 12th.

Pisces is the Cuspe of the 6th. Her disease came by wet taken at the feet. Jupiter in Virgo gave corruption in blood, and informities in the bowels; with what they were, more anon.

Venus with the Scorpions heart skews a violent Fever; neither proved it to be any lesse.

The Sun and Mars in the Fourth house with the Dragons tail in Quartile to the ascendent, shew violence in the disease, danger of poyson, and an ill end of it; her Physitian is signified by Mars, which was a French Quack which lay in the house, and he was as like Mars ,in Capricorn, as a Pomewater is to an Apple.

He was always troubled with sore eyes, a man of forlorn fortunes; view the position of Mars and you shall easily see the reason without a pair of spectacles.

The position of Mars in the Fourth combust with the Dragons-tail, and in the Quartile of the ascendent, First, clouded his judgement; secondly, corrupted his practice; Thirdly, set hard for her life.

'Tis a sad thing when the Lord of Death must be the Physitian in the disease.

Her disease was the small pox, in which being exceedingly bound in her body, not going to stool in a week together and above; he plied her all that time with strong purges (ob acute Physitian!) never one of them working, nor so much as coming from her; though there was SCAMMONY in every one of them; that had not I so soon as I knew of it perswaded her Nurse to give her Clyster ever day, and she had absolutely perished; her purges increasing her Fever, and poysoning her body, and this I am confident was the reason both of her being so much disfigured by her disease, and of her aches and swellings in the knees; (for Mars was in Capricorn) which continued upon her until her dying day, which followed about a year and a half after. Neither was her Doctor's judgement one jot inferiour to his practice: for in the beginning of the disease, viz. the next day after she fell sick, came accidentally to the house, and found all the household weeping; every one that could eat an egg, shed a tear. A Joyner was busie pulling down the bed-steds, the whole household preparing for a flight with bag and baggage.

And what was the reason, think you ? The Doctor had passed a wild piece of Non-sense that she was got the Pestilence, and was full of the tokens; up run I to see the creature; I found her in a strong Fever, that's true; But I could see no tokens, unlesse 'twere tokens of the Doctor's ingnorance I demanded the time of her falling sick, which she very exactly gave me. And having taken the pains to erect the figure, I did what I could to cherish up her spirits. I told her, my judgement was, that she would live. I certified the household that she had no such disease as Pestilence, much lesse any tokens. And thus whoever lost, the Joyner he got by the bargain on both hands; First, pulling the bed-steds and tables to pieces, and for setting them together again. And thus you see, 'tis an ill wind that blows no body no profit.

I have but two questions to answer, and then I come to the Crisis,

1. Will she live or die ?

2. Will her sicknesse be long or short ?

To the first of these I answer; That Mars is Lord of death, and also an afflicting Planet, in trine to the Lord of the Sixth, and in Sextile to the Moon, with the Sun are in Quartile to the Ascendent; this is all the signs of death, that is, besides the great sign (viz.) her Doctor swore she would die, and could not possibly live; having as the Coxcomb said, not so much of her lungs left, as amounted to the quantity of three of her fingers; a likely tale forsooth, was it not?

I was a diligent observer of every passage of this sicknesses and I found it always true, that during her sicknesse, the Moon by transit to the body or beams of Mars afflicted her sorely.

But not so, to the beams of Saturn; for that only possessed her body with coldnesse and chillinesse.

That she should live, is very clear; the Moon being with the Sextile of Jupiter, and the Lord of the Ascendant no way afflicted, save only by the Scorpions heart.

To the Second Question, namely, whether her disease should be long or short;

The Angles being all Cardinal, and the Moon swift in motion, and in Sextile to Jupiter, shew a short sickness; The Lord of the Ascendant, and the Lord of the Sixth being both stationary, prolong the disease.

And indeed though the disease taken under the notion of acute, were long, yet taken according to reason, it is shorter then could be imagined.

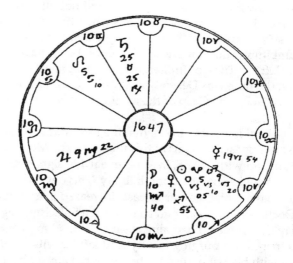

The first judicial time is when the Moon comes to 10° 40' Sagitarius. It is called a judicial because at that time the disease appears in his colours, that a man may know what it tends to.

The second time which you may find upon the third house in the Critical Figure, is called intercidental, because it falls between the judicial and Critical times; and upon this intercidental time, there is usually some remission of the disease, that so nature may have time to rally up her forces against her encounter with the disease on her Crisis. And according as it falls out upon the intercidental time either to good or bad, so a good or bad Crisis may be expected. But to return: the Moon comes to Sagittarius 10° 40' upon the 14th of December, about a half an hour after six in the Morning. If you please but to set the figure, you shall find she is just upon the Cusp in the ascendant, newly separated from the body of Venus, and the Quartile of Jupiter: now the small pox came out, and not till now. The first intercidental time happens when the Moon comes to 10° 40' of Capricorn, the place where Mars was at the Decumbiture, and now she applies to his body, having newly left the Trine of Jupiter. If you please to set the Figure, the time was December 16th. 1 hour 24 minutes, P.M. Saturn is upon the Cusp of the ascendant: about this time she got cold.

And I am of opinion, that the ascendant and sixth House being earthly signs at this time, and the Moon in Conjunction with MARS, in another earthly sign, doth clearly shew her being bound in body. This day, which should have mitigated her disease, increased it; and now her Doctor (if I may call him so without a Solecism) begins to play the antique, I had almost said, the mad man. Now he exerciseth his purging faculty, and left his wits a bed and asleep with his last night's Mistresse. Sure I am, a Physician would admire to hear SCAMMONY given to a creature that had the small pox coming out upon her. To conclude, a very ill Crisis is threatened.

The first Crisis comes about, upon the 18th of December, three quarters of an hour past 11, of night; the face of heaven is not much altered from what it was at the Decumbiture. The Moon separates from the Sextile of

Venus, Lady of the ascendant, and applyes to the Quartile of Saturn; and had Doctor Dunce only judged she would have died now, as indeed he did, he might have been pardoned, although he had fail'd; but also, he poor man, had little skill in times and seasons; his skill was employed to know a woman from a man, when he had got her in bed. He did not only say, but also swore, that she would die about the intercidental time, though such a thing be seldom seen in a man's age; but let us to our Art, and let the Doctor's ignorance alone.

You shall find, if you please to set the positions of Heaven, the Scheme almost the same with that of the Decumbiture; the Moon carries the beams of the Lady of the ascendant to the Quartile of Saturn. The Sun and Mars cast hurtful beams to the ascendant; and indeed my own opinion is, that had the Moon applied to MARS, as she did to SATURN, it had kill'd her.

Howsoever, the premises considered, it is clear, that this is likely to be the time of greatest danger in all her sicknesses and so indeed it was. Now must the disease needs be strongest, nature weakest; and if this time be past the bitterness of death is past. Indeed at this time, the combat was fore, the distracted, senselesse, the small pox began to fall down; and withal, strength almost spent; but above all, the Doctor swore she could not live while morning.

Rational hopes of her life are the dignities of SATURN in the ascendant, bur especially the Trine of the Sun and JUPITER upon that day. It is the opinion of the learned in this Art, that let the Significators of life or death seated or disposed as badly as they can be; yet if Sun be in Conjunction or good aspect with JUPITER, the sick will live; and truly so did she, almost to admiration.

But some will ask, and 'tis a question' worth the answering; that if the Sun and JUPITER preserve life, as they say, when they are so seated, what's the reason men die at that time ? for we see men die dayly.

To this I answer briefly, that truly in the nativity of some people, JUPITER is the killing Planet; and in the sickness of such sick persons, JUPITER will as soon kill as SATURN and MARS; every Planet must do his office: I proceed

The second judicial time comes about the 21st of December, at noon, or a very little after; at which time Mars is Lord of the ascendant, strong, and in hi.s exaltation.

The Moon having left the Sextile of the Sun,applies to his Sextile. The face of heaven is quiet and clean altered from what it was at the Decumbiture; a manifest sign of some change. Besides, though Saturn be in the ascendant, and Mars in the 10th House; yet Jupiter is in the 6th, therefore some good may be hoped; I do not know that it is besides the rule of Art, if I should affirm that as Mars in the 4th House of the Decumbiture kept her Doctors (you may call it folly), or madnesse (which you please) close, so now in the 10th House reveals it. Now, and not till now did I know of her Doctor's frantick course of Physick, and of her not going to stool: from this time she took a Clyster every day until she amended.

The second Crisis comes upon the Sun the 26th of December, about one hour after noon; at which time the Moon 1S Strong in her own exaltation, and applies to the Trine of the Sun and Mercury; at this time her fever left her, and she began to recover: And upon the third Crisis, which happened upon the first of January, she went abroad.

Chapter VIII.
To find the exact time of the Crisis by a Table of Logistical Logarithmes.

Seeing that many are unskilful in finding, or calculating the true time of the Crisis after Decumbiture; I have in this Edition inserted a Table by which it may be easily performed, if the following Rules be duly observed; (and if they be not, I cannot help it).

In the head of the Table is placed the 24 hours of the natural day, which also serve for degrees, as occasion serveth. In the little Colume to the left hand are placed the minutes, as is usual in other Tables; in the greater Columes are placed the LOGISTICAL LOGARITHMES of any hour and minute of the natural day, &c.

When you would find the LOGISTICAL LOGARITHME of any hour and minute, or Degree and minute, seek the hour or degree in the head, and the minutes in the side, and at the angle of meeting you have the same.

Example

I would know the LOGISTICAL LOGARITHMS of 6 hours 40 minutes, I seek for 6 at the head of the dexter page, and for 40 in the side, and at the angle of meeting, I have 12809, the LOGIS. LOGAR. Thereof.

When you have a LOGARITHMS, and would know the hours and minutes belonging thereto seek the same at the nearest thereto (for that will serve very well) in the Table, and at the head of the colume where you find it, you have the hour, and then cast your eye to the little colume on the left hand, and you have the minutes.
Example.

I would know what hours and minutes this LOGARITHME 9025 doth belong to; having found the same in the Table, at the head of that column where I find it, is placed 9 and against it in the side
44. viz. 9 hours 44 minutes.
(See Logistical Logarithme Table

Having the hour and minute of the Decumbiture, find the places of the Planets for that time. In the Ephemeris you have their places every day at noon.
When Planets are direct, subtract their place the day precedent, from their place the day subsequent, and you have their diurnal motions; but when they are retrograde,

subtract their place the subsequent day, from their place the precedent day, and you have likewise their diurnal motions. Unless the Logistical Logarithme of the hours and minutes, afternoon of the Decumbiture, add severally the Logistical Logarithme of the Planets diurnal motions, and the sums shall be the Logistical Logarithm of the proportional degree or minute: which when Planets are direct (the Sun and Moon are always so, if you call your self to remembrance) must be added to their place the day precedent; but when they are retrograde, it must be subtracted from their place the day precedent, and their aggregate of remainder will be their true place at the Decumbiture.

Having found the Moons place at the Decumbiture, by adding 45° thereto, you have her place at the first judicial time; by adding three signs to her place at the Decumbiture, you have her place at the first Crisis; and so by a continual addition of 45°, the Moons place at the Crisis and judicial days is found, as is shewed in Chapter 5.

Observe in the Ephemeris what day the Moon's place is next lesse then her place at the Crisis, or judicial day and note the difference; and also note the diurnal motion that day. Then from the Logistical Logarithm of the difference of the Moon's place at noon that day, and her place at the Crisis, subtract the Logistical Logarithm of her diurnal motion, and the remainder will be the Logistical Logarithm of the time after noon, of the Crisis, or judicial day.

Example.
A man fell sick of Fever, 1652, November 7th, being Sunday at 8 & 10 minutes at night. At which time he was taken with a great horrour, and with shaking, as in a violent Ague, &c. In my Ephemeris for that year, you will find (if you look) the Planets places upon the 7th and 8th days of that month, as followeth

	☉	☽	♄	♃	♂	♀	☿

	♏	♊	♌	♐	♎	♎	♏
7th	25 04	20 31	13 02	11 45	0 47	12 30	18 34
8th	26 05	4 04	13 03	11 57	1 23	14 08	20 12

Then subtract their places the 7th day from their places the
8th day, because they are all direct, and the diurnal motion
will be

	☉	☽	♄	♃	♂	♀	☿
	1 01	13 33	0 01	0 12	0 36	0 38	1 38

The Logistical Logarithm of 8 hours 10 minutes is 10780
which is added unto the Logistical Logarithm of the Planets
diurnal motion, the work will be as in the following
examples-

    1 01' Sun's diurnal motion   31616
Log. Log. of 8h 10m time afternoon   10780

        0°21' to be added   4236

to 25°49' which will produce the Sun's Place in 26° 10' of
Scorpio.

                  13°33' diur. mot Moon   5716
Log. Log. of   8h 10m time afternoon   10780

                  4°37' to be added   16496

to 20°Gemini, the Moon's place on the 7th day, which will
make 25°Gemini 08' her place at the Decumbiture.
If you deal after the same manner with the rest of the
Planets, as in these two examples of the Sun and Moon,
their places at the Decumbiture will be,

☉	☽	♄	♃	♂	♀	☿
♏	♊	♌	♐	♎	♎	♏
26 10	25 08	13 02	11 40	0 59	12 43	19 03

Then the first judicial day will be when the Moon cometh to 10° 08' of Leo on the 10th day of the same month. Moon's place is 29° 52' of Cancer being the next lesse, and wanteth of 10° 08' in Leo, 10° 16', and her diurnal motion is 12° 27'.

	10°16' the difference	8491
Logis. Log. of	12°27' the diurn. mot	6563

	19h 48m the time	1928

afternoon that the first judicial day falleth on, viz. the 11th day at 7h and 48 m in the morning.

The first Crisis happeneth when the Moon cometh to 25° 08' Virgo on the 14th day, the Moon's place in 19° 44' Virgo and wanteth of 25° 08', 5° 24'. Her diurnal motion is 11° 55'

	5°24' the difference	14916
Logis. Log. of	11°55' the diurn. mot	7001

	10h53m the time	7915

afternoon of the first Crisis, viz. at 10 o'clock and 53 minutes at night, the 14th day of November.

The second Crisis will be when the Moon cometh to 25° 08' of Sagittarius, the 21st day. Moon's place is 14° 50' in Sagittarius and wanteth of 25° 08' (the place of the Crisis) 10° 18' and her diurnal motion is 12° 40'.

	10°18' the difference	8459
Logis. Log. of	12°40' the diurn. mot	6391

	19h31m the time	2008

of the second Crisis afternoon, viz. at half an hour after 7 in the morning, the 22nd day.

The like method used in the other, as in these examples; the Moon's place, and time, &c. will be as in the following Synopsis.

A Synopsis of the Whole Calculation

CRITICAL DATES	Moon's Place	TIME OF INCIDENCE		The Lunar Aspects and the mutual aspects of the Planets
Decumbiture	25 Gremini 08	Nov 7	8hr10am	square Saturn, Mercury Moon to square Mars
1st Judic.	10 Leo 08	11th	71h48am	Sextile Saturn, Venus Moon to sextile Venus
1st Crisis	25 Virgo 08	14th	1053pm	Moon to sextile Mercury approaching S. Node
2 Judic.day	10 Scorpio 08	18th	5 02pm	Moon to square Saturn and sextile Jupiter. sextile Sun, Mars
2nd Crisis	25 Sagitarius 08	22nd	7 31 am	Moon to square Mars trine Sun, Saturn
3rd Judic.	10 Aquarius 08	25th	4 01pm	Moon to oppos. Saturn and trine Mars. Conj. Sun, Venus.
3rd Crisis	25 Pisces 08	28th	8 51 pm	Moon with N. Node, he recovers
4th Judic.	10 Taurus 08	Dec 1st	6 37 pm	
4 Crisis	25 Gemini 08	5th	4 52 am	

	A Table of Logistical Logarithms.										
	0	1	2	3	4	5	6	7	8	9	10
0	Infini:31780:24849:20794:17917:15686:13863:13231:10986:9808:8755:
1	72723:31616:24766:20739:17876:15653:13835:12298:10965:9790:8738:
2	65792:31953:24689:20684:17835:15620:13807:12274:10944:9771:8721:
3	62327:31294:24602:20629:17793:15587:13780:12250:10924:9753:8705:
4	58861:31135:24521:20575:17752:15554:13752:12227:10906:9734:8688:
5	56834:30981:24441:20520:17711:15521:13725:12201:10882:9716:8672:
6	54806:30827:24361:20466:17671:15488:13698:12179:10862:9698:8655:
7	53367:30678:24281:20413:17630:15455:13670:12156:10841:9679:8639:
8	51930:30526:24204:20359:17590:15423:13643:12133:10821:9661:8622:
9	50814:30384:24126:20307:17558:15391:13616:12109:10800:9643:8606:
10	49699:30239:24049:20254:17509:15358:13589:12086:10780:9625:8589:
11	48787:30098:23972:20201:17469:15326:13562:12063:10759:9607:8573:
12	47875:29957:23896:20149:17430:15294:13535:12040:10739:9588:8557:
13	47104:29820:23821:20097:17390:15262:13509:12017:10719:9570:8540:
14	46335:29684:23740:20045:17351:15230:13481:11993:10699:9552:8529:
15	45666:29550:23672:19994:17311:15198:13455:11970:10678:9534:8508:
16	44998:29417:23597:19943:17272:15166:13428:11947:10658:9516:8491:
17	44409:29287:23524:19892:17233:15125:13402:11925:10638:9498:8975:
18	43820:29157:23451:19841:17194:15103:13375:11902:10618:9480:8459:
19	43393:29030:23375:19791:17156:15072:13349:11879:10598:9462:8443:
20	42767:28904:23307:19741:17117:15041:13326:11856:10578:9445:8427:
21	42290:28780:23237:19691:17079:15010:13296:11833:10558:9427:8411:
22	41814:28657:23166:19641:17040:14978:13270:11811:10538:9409:8394:
23	41279:28536:23096:19591:17002:14947:13244:11788:10518:9391:8378:
24	40943:28416:23026:19543:16964:19916:13218:11766:10498:9373:8362:
25	40543:28278:22957:19495:16927:14886:13191:11793:10478:9356:8346:
26	40154:28182:22881:19445:16889:14855:13166:11721:10459:9338:8330:
27	39772:28066:22820:19397:16852:14824:13140:11698:10439:9320:8314:
28	39402:27951:22752:19349:16814:14794:13114:11676:10419:9303:8298:
29	39057:27838:22671:19301:16777:14763:13088:11654:10399:9285:8289:
30	38712:27726:22618:19253:16740:14733:13062:11631:10380:9268:8267:

	A Table of Logistical Logarithms.										
	0	1	2	3	4	5	6	7	8	9	10
31	38394:27616:22551:19205:16703:14703:13037:11609:10360:9250:8256:										
32	38067:27506:22485:19158:16666:14673:13011:11587:10341:9232:8235:										
33	37764:27399:22420:19102:16629:14643:12986:11565:10321:9215:8219:										
34	37460:27291:22354:19069:16593:19613:12960:11543:10302:9198:8204:										
35	37179:27186:22290:19018:16556:14583:12935:11521:10282:9180:8188:										
36	36889:27080:22225:18971:16519:14553:12972:11499:10263:9163:8172:										
37	36613:26997:22152:18925:16984:14529:12885:71477:10243:9196:8156:										
38	36348:26874:22068:18879:I6448:14994:12859:11455:10224:9128:8191:										
39	36092:26773:22035:18833:I6412:14464:12834:11433:10205:9111:8125:										
40	35835:26672:21972:18788:16376:14435:12809:11412:10186:9094:8109:										
41	35591:26573:21910:18792:16391:14405:12784:11390:10166:9077:8094:										
42	35347:26474:21818:18697:16305:14376:12759:11368:10147:9059:8078:										
43	35115:26377:21787:18652:16269:14347:12735:11347:10128:9042:8062:										
44	34882:26280:21725:18607:16134:14318:12710:11325:10109:9025:8047:										
45	39660:26185:21665:18563:16199:19289:12685:11304:10090:9008:8031:										
46	34937:26089:21604:18519:16169:14260:12660:11282:10071:8991:8016:										
47	34225:25996:21544:18474:16129:14231:12636:11261:10052:8974:8001:										
48	34012:25903:21989:18930:16094:14202:12611:11239:10033:8957:7985:										
49	33806:25817:21925:18387:16060:14173:12587:11218:10014:8940:7970:										
50	33604:25719:21306:19343:16025:14145:12562:11197:9995:8923:7954:										
51	33398:25629:21307:18300:15991:14116:12593:11175: 9976:8909:7939:										
52	33211:25530:21249:18257:15956:14088:12514:11154: 9957:8889:7923:										
53	33023:25450:21191:18214:15922:14059:12989:11133: 9939:8872:7908:										
54	32834:25362:21133:18171:15888:14031:12465:11112: 9920:8855:7893:										
55	32652:25275:21076:18129:15854:14003:12441:11091: 9901:8838:7878:										
56	32470:25188:21019:18086:15820:13975:12417:11070: 9883:8821:7862:										
57	32295:25103:20963:18043:15787:13997:12393:11099: 9864:8805:7847:										
58	32119:25017:20906:18001:15753:13919:12369:11028: 9845:4788:7832:										
59	31950:24939:20850:17959:15720:13891:12345:11007: 9827:8771:7817:										
60	31780:24849:20794:17917:15686:13863:12321:10986: 9808:8755:7801:										

	A Table of Logistical Logarithms.												
	11	12	13	14	15	16	17	18	19	20	21	22	23
0	7801	6931	6131	5390	4700	4055	3448	2377	2336	1823	1335	870	425
1	7786	6918	6118	5378	4689	4014	3425	2867	2327	1816	1327	852	418
2	7771	6904	6105	5366	4678	4034	3429	2858	2319	1807	1319	855	411
3	7756	6890	6093	5359	4667	4023	3419	2849	2310	1798	1312	897	401
4	7791	6876	6080	5342	4656	4013	3409	2840	2301	1790	1309	840	397
5	7726	6862	6067	5331	4695	4003	3's99	2831	2292	1733	1296	832	339
6	7711	6848	6054	5319	4634	3992	3390	2821	2284	1773	1288	825	382
7	7696	6835	6092	5307	4623	3982	3380	2812	2275	1765	1280	817	375
8	7681	6821	6029	5295	4612	3972	3370	2803	2266	1757	1272	810	368
9	7666	6807	6016	5283	4600	3961	3360	2799	2257	1748	1264	802	361
10	7651	6793	6004	5272	4589	3951	3351	2785	2249	1740	1256	795	353
11	7636	6779	5991	5260	4578	3941	3341	2775	2240	1732	1248	787	318
12	7621	6765	5978	5248	9567	3930	3331	2766	2231	1724	1240	780	339
13	7606	6752	5966	5236	4557	3920	3322	2757	2223	1715	1233	772	332
14	7592	6738	5953	5225	4546	3910	3312	2718	2214	1707	1225	765	325
15	7277	6725	5990	5213	4535	3900	3302	2739	2205	1699	1217	757	317
16	7562	6712	5928	5201	4524	3889	3293	2730	2197	1691	1209	750	310
17	7547	6693	5915	5190	4513	3379	3233	2721	2188	1682	1201	792	303
18	7532	6684	5903	5178	4502	3669	3273	2771	2179	1674	1193	735	296
19	7518	6671	5890	5166	4491	3859	3264	2702	2171	1666	1186	727	239
20	7503	6657	5878	5155	4480	3848	3254	2693	2162	1658	1178	720	232
21	7483	6644	5865	5143	4469	3838	3245	2684	2154	1650	1170	712	273
22	7479	6630	5853	5131	4458	3828	3235	2675	2145	1641	1162	705	267
23	7459	6617	5840	5120	4448	3318	3225	2666	2136	1633	1159	697	260
24	7444	6604	5828	5108	4437	3804	321E	2657	2129	1625	1147	690	253
25	7430	6590	5815	5097	4426	3797	3206	2648	2119	1617	1139	682	246
26	7415	6577	5803	5085	4415	3787	3197	2639	2111	1609	1131	675	239
27	7401	6563	5791	5074	4404	3777	3167	2630	2102	1601	1123	668	232
28	7386	6550	5778	5062	4394	3767	3177	2621	2093	1592	1116	660	225
29	7372	6537	5766	5050	4383	3757	3168	2612	2085	1581	1108	653	218
30	7357	6523	5751	5039	4372	3717	3158	2603	2076	1576	1100	645	210

	A Table of Logistical Logarithms.												
	11	12	13	14	15	16	17	18	19	20	21	22	23
31	7342	6511	5741	5027	4361	3737	3149	2594	2068	1568	1092	638	203:
32	7328	6497	5729	5016	4351	3727	3139	2585	2059	1560	1084	630	196:
33	7319	6483	5716	5005	4340	3717	3130	2576	2051	1552	1077	623	189:
34	7299	6970	5704	4993	4329	3707	3120	2567	2042	1544	1069	616	182:
35	7285	6457	5692	4982	4318	3696	3111	2558	2034	1536	1061	608	175:
36	7270	6444	5680	4970	4308	3686	3101	2549	2025	1528	1054	601	168:
37	7256	6330	5668	4959	4297	3676	3092	2540	2017	1520	1046	594	161:
38	7242	6417	5655	4947	4286	3666	3083	2531	2008	1511	1038	586	154:
39	7227	6404	5643	4936	4276	3656	3073	2522	2000	1503	1030	579	197:
40	7213	6391	5631	4925	4265	3646	3064	2513	1991	1495	1023	571	140:
41	7199	6378	5619	4913	4254	3636	3054	2504	1983	1487	1015	569	133:
42	7185	6364	5607	4902	4249	3626	3045	2395	1974	1479	1007	557	126:
43	7170	6351	5599	4891	4233	3616	3035	2486	1966	1471	1000	549	119:
44	7156	6338	5582	4879	4223	3606	3026	2477	1957	1463	992	542	112:
45	7142	6320	5570	4868	4212	3596	3017	2469	1949	1455	984	535	105:
46	7128	6312	5558	4857	4201	3587	3007	2460	1940	1447	977	527	98:
47	7114	6299	5546	4845	4190	3577	2998	2451	1932	1439	969	520	91:
48	7099	6286	5534	4834	4180	3567	2988	2442	1924	1431	961	513	84:
49	7085	6273	5522	4823	4170	3557	2979	2433	1915	1423	954	506	77:
50	7071	6260	5510	4812	4160	3547	2970	2424	1907	1415	946	498	70.
51	7057	6247	5198	4800	4149	3537	2960	2415	1898	1407	938	491	63:
52	7043	6234	5486	4789	4138	3527	2951	2407	1890	1399	931	484	56:
53	7029	6221	5174	4778	4128	3517	2942	2398	1882	1391	923	476	49:
54	7015	6208	5462	4767	4117	3507	2932	2389	1873	1382	916	969	42:
55	7001	6195	5450	4756	4108	3497	2923	2380	1865	1375	908	462	35:
56	6987	6782	5433	4744	4096	3488	2914	2371	1857	1367	900	455	28.
57	6973	6169	5426	4733	4086	3478	2905	2362	1848	1359	893	447	21:
58	6959	6157	5414	4722	4075	3468	2895	2354	1840	1351	885	440	14:
59	6945	6144	5402	4711	4065	3458	2886	2345	1831	1344	878	433	7:
60	6931	6131	5390	4700	4055	3448	2877	2336	1823	1335	870	425	0

Liber II

Chapter IX.

Certain Precepts premised before the Prognosticks.

First of all take notice that the Significators of Diseases are to be taken under these two notions. 1. General, or more principal. 2. Particular, or lesse principal: The general or more principal are these, the Sun, the Moon, and the Ascendant; of these the Sun is most principally to be looked upon in Chronick diseases, the Moon in Acute.

Significators particular or lesse principal are these:

1. The Lord of the Ascendant.
2. The sixth House.
3. The Lord of the sixth House.
4. The Planets in the Ascendant or sixth House.
5. SATURN and MARS; for they naturally hurt the body, whatsoever the matter is.

2. The sixth House and its Lord, and the Planets in it, if there be any there, best describe the nature of the disease usually, nay always, if they afflict either of the Luminaries, or the Lord of the Ascendant.

3. The Aspects of the Moon to the Planets are always to be noted; for they produce something to the sick, but especially upon Critical and Judicial days; for you shall find this a certain truth, even as certain as the Sun, (and he never fails without a miracle) That when the Moon passes by the bodies of JUPITER and VENUS, or their aspects, especially their good ones, if they be not Lords of death, she remits the most desperate symptoms in a sickness, and gives the sick some ease; as also the bodies or any aspect of SATURN to MARS exasperates a disease, and spoils the most hopeful symptoms.

4. Here then you have one way to do yourselves good.

A Physitian is Nature's helper, or at least he should be so; whosoever would help Nature, must of necessity be well acquainted with her; a little communication between them will instruct him the way and manner which Almighty

God bath allotted her to govern the world by; wisdom instructs her Children in the knowledge of time; for there is an appointed time for everything under the Sun; if then when a disease seems extream dangerous, you would make an essay to relieve languising Nature, do it at the time when the Moon passeth by the body, or good Aspect of JUPITER or VENUS, then its Nature in a capability of receiving help; you may before lift up a living man with one finger, then a dead man with both hands; a Bird while she bath wings can fly; but cut off her wings, and hang a couple of mill-stones on her legs, she cannot; Even so the bodies, and good Aspects of JUPITER and VENUS are like wings to carry men from a sicknesse to health.

The bodies and Aspects of SATURN and MARS, are like Mill-stones, to weigh him to his grave.

One thing more let me tell you, and I'll tell you but the truth; they say, if SATURN afflict JUPITER helps more then VENUS; but if MARS afflict VENUS helps more then JUPITER; let them say so still; but if you will be ruled by me, make use of that fortune which is strongest; a rich friend may relieve your wants, a poor friend cannot, he may wish you well, and so forth. But suppose you dare not stay while the Moon come to the good aspect of JUPITER and VENUS [When the Moon comes to that degree and minute and Sign Jupiter or Venus was in at the Decumbiture], administer your medicine when she is in the place where one of them was at the Decumbiture; if you dare not stay that time neither, one of them two in the Ascendant [viz. observe by the table of houses when Jupiter or Venus will crosse in the Ascendant] when you adminster the medicine. Put all these together, and it will tell you in words at length, and not in figures, That a Physitian without Astrology,is like a pudding without fat.

5. That place and state of the Planet from which the Moon is separated at the Decumbiture, and the condition the Planet also (for Planets are of different conditions as well as men, some good, and some bad) is to be heeded.

If you please to observe the state of that same Planet, by it you may know the state of the sick, and what the cause of his sickness is.

When you have done so, it is your wisest way to consider to what Planet the Moon applies; and then do but so much as view what sign that Planet is in, what his conditions be, whether he be benevolent or malevolent; whether he be Masculine or Feminine, Diurnal or Nocturnal, hot, dry, cold or moist; what part of the body he governs, and what disease he governs.

7. Consider whether the Planet the Moon applies to be in an Angle, in a succeeding, or in a cadent house; and when you have done so, do but so much as consider what the house he is in signifies, and what members of the body it governs; and then take but a little notice whether the Planet joy in the House or not; that you may not be mistaken herein, I will certifie you in what Houses every Planet takes his delight, as being confident, even amongst Astrologers, more are ignorant of it then know it.

1. The Sun delighteth in the fourth, ninth and eleventh houses.

2. The Moon rejoyceth in the third and seventh houses.

3. Saturn rejoyceth in the Ascendant, eighth and twelfth houses.

4. Jupiter rejoyceth in the second, ninth and eleventh.

5. Mars rejoyceth in the third, sixth and tenth.

6. Venus rejoyceth in the fifth and twelfth.

7. Mercury rejoyceth in the Ascendant and sixth.

Here's but a few words, yet so significant, that the nature and condition, the Sympathy and Antipathy of the Planets, and by consequence of the Creation, may be known from it: 'Tis not my present scope to tell you which way; whet your wits upon it, and they will be the sharper.

8. Consider whether the Planet the Moon applies to, be direct or retrograde; swift or slow in motion, Oriental,

Occidental, or Combust, whether fortunated, or infortunated by other Planets.

9. And when you have done so, it is your wisest way to consider whether the threatening Planet be in his own House or Exaltation, or other essential dignities, whether he be in Planets of good terms or evil; for if a good Planet have gotten an ill Planet in his Term, he will order him. To wind up this in one word, consider whether the threatening Planet have power to execute his will or not; for sometimes a curst cow hath short horns.

10. Do but so much as note what configurations the Lord of the Ascendant, six and eighth Houses have one with another; And amongst the rest, do not forget the Lord of the seventh and twelfth Houses, and I'll give you my reason why: The seventh, because it opposeth the Ascendant, he assaults life openly, and is not ashamed of what he doth: he plays the part of AJAX, goes to't with down-right blows without policy. The sixth, eighth and twelfth houses have no affinity at all with the Ascendant: And they have more of ULYSSES in them then AJAX; they take away a man's life when he's asleep, or else when lie knows not how.

11. Partile Aspects are far more strong and prevalent than platick.

12. Be please but to consider, that the sixth House, and his Lord, signifies the sickness: The seventh the Physitian: the eighth Death: the tenth the Medicine: the fourth the end of the Disease and when you have done so, I have done with this point.

These things thus premised, when you have read them, you shall find I first came to .....

Chapter X.
General Prognostications of the Diseases.

First of all (quoth my Author) The House of Heaven is of more force then the Sign; and it's very like; and the Sign then the Planet; and the Planet then the fixed Star he is with. But Doctor Reason told me, the Planet was of more force then the sign, because he was neerer to the earth.

    2. If the Ascendant, and the luminaries, and their Lords be afflicted by the Malevolent, or by an ill House, or by the Lord of Death, (it's no great matter what Star it is) and the benevolents lend no aid, 'tis shrewdly to be suspected the sicknesse drages death at's tail; he's a wise Physitian that can cut the cord.

    3. If the forenamed significators be well disposed, and not afflicted, the fear of death is more then the harm.

4. A benevolent Planet in the sixth, cures the disease without the help of a Physitian.

5. A Malevolent Planet there causeth a change in the disease, and usually from better to worse.

6. An infortune in the seventh shews but a Paltry Physitian, though he be a Collegiate. A fortune there, the contrary.

7. A fortune in the tenth shews proper physick, whosoever gives it.

8. A fortune in the fourth brings the disease to a good and speedy end (unless he be Lord of the Eighth.) Every man must do his office, and as the case may be ordered, JUPITER may kill a man as soon as SATURN.

9. JUPITER helps most in cold diseases, VENUS in hot.

10. The bodies of JUPITER and VENUS soon cure the sick; their Trines and Sextiles will not be much behind hand in the businesses And to tell you my own opinion without any compliments, The Quartile and oppositions of JUPITER and VENUS, is better then the Sextile and Trine of SATURN or MARS, in this case, [speaking in relation to the Moon in a Crisis, or otherwise] unlesse they be Lords of the Ascendant. And by the time you have been acquainted with Doctor Experience but half so long as I have been, he'll make you believe what I say is true.

11. A Malevolent in the Ascendant threatens death; and makes the sick as cross-grained as BAJAZET the Turkish Emperour when he was in the Iron Cage.

12. Good Stars in bad places, afflict the humour they govern: They do the like if they be afflicted with malevolent; was never any of you that reads these lines abused by honest people?

13. The conjunction of the Moon and MERCURY is as a weather-cock; the disposition of MERCURY is very various according to his position and aspect: with the Fortunes he is better then either; He's [viz. of the Fortunes, but I scarcely believe it] just like the people of this Nation; he follows the swinge of the times.

14. The Moon in conjunction with the Sun upon a Critical day, always portends mischief; and say, I told you of it; no Aspect is so propitious to the Moon as the Trine and Sextile of the Sun. Nothing so hateful to the squeamish Virgin as his Conjunction, Quartile and Opposition.

15. If the Moon upon a Critical day apply to a malevolent, you'll say that is but a scurvy sign; I am half of your opinion; yet it is good to be wise, and that you may be so, see which of them is strongest, the Moon or the Malevolent;

If the Moon be strongest, she'll make a handsome shift with him; if she be weakest, you know the old Proverb, THE WEAKEST GOES TO THE WALLS, and the sick is like to be forced to make use of a winding-sheet instead of a feather-bed.

16. If the Moon upon a Critical day be with the bodies of SOL, MARS or SATURN: and which of them she's withal, the Lord of the eighth House, away trots life to seek a new habitation, for she's weary of her old house.

17. If the Moon on a Critical day be strong in her house or exaltation, though aspected to no Planet at all, she'll play her part stoutly (for all she is a woman) that she'll restore the sick to his pristine health, if she were not too much afflicted in the Decumbiture.

18. If the Moon be not afflicted at the Decumbiture (as such a thing may be) yet if she be afflicted on the Critical day, a good Crisis cannot be expected: Sickness keeps his old house, unlesse death dispossesse him. This in general: But

he that would go with wisest way to work in judging of diseases, must come to particulars. The thing I promised you in this Chapter, was general Prognostications of diseases; which that I may make lucidly appear to you (for you shall not finde one of PHARAOHS Taskmasters of me, to set you to make bricks, and give you no straw;) be but pleased seriously to weigh in the ballance of Reason these particulars.

1. First of all, What diseases every Planet of himself distinctly causeth.

2. What diseases distinctly are under every several signs of the Zodiack.

3. What particular mart and member of the holy every Planet generally useth.

4. What particular part and member of the body is under the influence of every sign of the Zodiack, and house of the heveans in a Celestial Scheme.

5. What part of the body every Planet particularly rules, according to his transit through each sign.

Of all these in Order, and in the same Order they are set down; and if I should happen to be a little critical against my Author, who can helpe it ?

Chapter XI.
The diseases the Planets signifie.

1. The Sun causeth Pimples and Burles in the face, afflictions of the heart; Heart-burning, Tremblings, Faintings, Tympanies, sore Eyes, and diseases of the mouth; Cramps, Convulsions, all diseases of the Heart and Brain, and their attendants, viz. the Nerves and Arteries, stinking breath, Catharrs, rotten Feavers; thus Authors. And if any aske why I mention no more, tell them here's more then is true. Now to the purpose.

First of all Tympanies are under the Moon: I have known the Sun give a fiery disease, but never a watry.

2. Cramps and Convulsions are under the Moon; and so are all diseases that often return, as agues do: you shall find the

same in another Aphorism afterwards; and although my Author contradict himself, I do not delight to imitate him in that sport.

3. The head, brain, and nerves, are under the Sun, as you shall hear hereafter.

4. Catharrs are under either MERCURY or JUPITER, or both; take this for a Maxime of truth, and say I told you so. A Planet ruling a part of the body, if he be weak in the Genesis, that part of the body is naturally weak; I confesse I know not wherefore Art was made but to help nature. The eyes are under the Luminaries, and whosoever hath them weak in the Genesis, hath but weak sight. The lungs are under JUPITER; MERCURY is the opposite Planet to JUPITER: Now then, if JUPITER be weak, he is not able to strengthen the Lungs as he should do; if MERCURY be the afflicting Planet, he weakens the lungs by opposition, if you have but wit enough to know by a penny how a shilling's coyned.

SENSIBUS HAEC (RES NOT EST PARMA) REPONE. *Afford these lines a place amidst your senses, And be not gull'd by specious pretences.*

I have now leaped from the Sun to the Moon, and she (they say) causeth Apoplexies, Palsies, Cholick, Belly-ach, diseases in the stones, Bladder, & instruments of Generation; stopping and overflowing of the Termes in Women, Dropsies, Fluxies [Tympanies, Diary Agues], all cold and Rhumatick diseases, Gout, Sciatica, Wormes in the Belly, Rhumes, and hurts in the Eyes, Surfeits, rotten Coughes, Convulsions, Falling-sicknesse, King's Evil, Aposthumrs, small Pox, and Measles; all coagulate and crude humours in any part of the body, Lethargies, and all diseases of Flegme; thus my Author.

Amongst these I except,

1. Apoplexies, and you shall find my reason within a quarter of an hour, unlesse you fall asleep with reading.

2. Diseases in the instruments of Generation; for they are caused by VENUS and MARS; by the one by Sympathy; by the other by Antipathy.

3. The Gout is caused by SATURNE. Who knows bur that's the reason, because he moves so slowly?

Now I must leave the Moon, and mount up to SATURNE; for I am like the world, never in a Station.

Under SATURNE, say Authors, are Apoplexies, Tooth-ach, Quartain Agues; all diseases whichcome of Melancholy, cold and drynesse, Leprosie, Rhumes, Consumhtisns, Black-Jaundice, Palsies, Trembling, vain feares, formidable fancies of a Hobgobling, Dropsi es, Gouts of all sorts; a Dog-like-hunger, Hemarrhoids, broken bones, and dislocations, deafnesse; pain in the bones: Ruptures if he be in Leo or Scorpio, or in an ill aspect to VENUS: Iliack passion, Chin-cough, Catharrs, pains in the bladder; all long diseases, all madnesse that comes of melancholy, fear or grief.

If you will give me leave (after I have been first a little Critical) I will be (secondly) a little instructive.

1. I except against Apoplexies; and if you would learn why, you shall, so soon as you have learned a little patience.

2. I except against Dropsies; for they are under the Moon.

3. I except against Catharrs, for they are under JUPITER'or MERCURY, or both.

4. I except against Dog-like hunger, for it's under MARS'

A few instructions would I willingly give you, if I thought you would be so wise to heed them. I had as good give them you under SATURNE, as under another Planet. I will not give them you under each Planet, because he's a foolish Musician that harps alwayes on one string.

A Planet causeth disease.

1. By Sympathy.

2. By Antipathy.

And as the cause is, so must the cure be, unlesse you will do as Scogging did, strike him that stands next you, because another abuses you.

These diseases SATURNE causeth by Sympathy; Tooth-ach, broken bones; the reason is because he rules the bones. Deafnesse he causeth because he rules the eares. Melancholy and all diseases of the spleen by the same argument. [Ergo the Spleen is the seat of Melancholy] 2. Also he afflicts all parts of the body that are under the Moon by antipathy; and likewise he plays the same tricks with those that are under the Sun; you shall know what they are by and by.
[Vide. N. C. Epicid. Phy. p 24 where you have directions for the cure of a disease Astrologically worth your noting.] The great wisdom of a Physitian is to know whether SATURNE cause the disease by Sympathy or Antipathy, and then take notice, that as the cause is, so is the cure, Sympathetical, or antipathetical; and withal do not forget, that sympathetical cures strengthen nature; Antipathetical cures, in one degree or another weaken it; and now you own mother-wit (if you have any) will teach you that Antipathetical Medicins are not to be used, unlesse to such Patients whom Doctor Ignorance or Doctor Carelessness hath had so long in hand, that Sympathetical will not serve the turn. To bring all this to the point in hand that so it may be useful: if SATURNE cause the disease by Sympathy, cure it by the Sympathetical herbs of SATURN. If he cause the disease by Antipathy, note whether it be Antipathy to Sun or Moon; or if it happen to the instruments of generation, be sure it is by Antipathy to VENUS. Make use of the Sympathetical herbs of those Planets for cure: [Viz. VENUS. For Sympathetical herbs of VENUS cure the diseases caused by the Antipathy of SATURN. Viz. You shall know what pills the part affected belong to, if you consider what precedes, and if SATURN be the cause of any disease in the Genitals, it's Antipathy to VENUS; if in the Spleen, then it's by Sympathy to himself, if the disease be caused by

Sympathy in any party by SATURNE; as the Lion to any
other Planet, is JUPITER to any disease in the Lungs; use the
Sympathetical herbs of JUPITER]: you shall not live the age
of a little fish, before I give you rational instructions for
them all: I now leave SATURN, and come a little lower to
JUPITER.

JUPITER they say causeth Apoplexies, all infirmities
of the Liver and Veins, inflammation of the Lungs, Plurisies,
and other Aposthumes about the Breast and Ribs, all
diseases proceeding of putrefaction of blood and wind,
quinsies, feavers, and other diseases; which Authors either
for want of wit, or super-abundance of ignorance are
pleased to attribute to him.

But I suppose JUPITER governs Apoplexies, because
it proceeds of Flegm; JUPITER governing the Lungs, and so
consequent of Flegm.

Against these I except.
1. Against Apoplexies; for it can not come about that all the
Planets should cause Apoplexies; if so, they would be more
frequent then they are: No good Argument.
2. Against corruption of blood: For SATURN corrupts the
blood by melancholy, and MARS choler.

MARS. Diseases under MARS are pestilences,
burning feavers, Teritan and quotidian agues, Megrim,
Carbuncles and Plague sores; Burning, Scalding,
Ring-worms, Blisters, Phrensie, Fury, Hair-braines, sudden
distempers in the head coming of heat: yellow jaundice,
Bloody-flux, Fistulas. All wounds whatsoever: Diseases in
the instruments of Generation: the stone in the reins and
bladder: scars and pockholes in the face: all hurts by Iron
and fire; the Shingles, Falling-sicknesse, Calentures, St.
Antbonies fire; all diseases coming of cboler, anger or
passion.

Amongst all these I can justly except but against
one: and that is the falling sickness, which is under the
Moon. And your self will be on my opinion if you please but

to take notice that those hideous fits usually come at conjunction, opposition, and quartile of the Moon to the Sun.

VENUS. Diseases under VENUS are all diseases of the wombe whatsoever, as Suffocation, Precipitation, dislocation, &c. All diseasesincident to the members of generation, the Refines and Navel, as the running of the Refines, the French Pox, &c. All diseases coming by inordinate love of lust, priapismus, impotency in the act of generation, ruptures of all sorts: All diseases belonging to the urine, as Disuria, Iscuria, and Stranguria, Iliack passion, Diabetes &c.

Against I except;
1. Impotency in the act of generation, for that's SATURNE.
2. Ruptures, for he bath a share in them also.
3. Diseases of the Urine, for they are under MARS.
4. The Iliack passion, which is under MERCURY.

MERCURY. Under MERCURY are almost all the diseases of the brain, as Vertigo, Madnesse, &c., all diseases of the Lungs, as Asthma, Phthisicks, &c. All imperfections of the Tongue, as Stammering, Lisping, &c. Hoarsenesse, Coughs, Snuffling in the head, Dumbnesse, Folly and simplicity (the Epidemical diseases of the time) and whatsoever hurts the intellectual faculty.

Against these I except.
1. Against the defects of memory, for SATURN has a great share in that.
2. Against the Gout, for SATURN wholly rules that.
I have now done with this part, and if any youngsters ask why I have not given a Reason for all I have spoken: Tell them the Reason is clear in the matter: and he that is not able to see it, is as unfit to give Physick. A blind man cannot see the Sun in a clear day when he is upon the Meridian.

PART II.

What diseases distinctly are under every signe of the Zodiack.

1. Under ARIES are all pushes, whelks, and pimples, freckles and Sun-burning in the face; the small Pox and Measles, Polypus, or NOLI ME TANGERE; all diseases in the Head, as the Head-ach of all- sorts, Vertigo, Frenzy, Lethargy, Forgetfulness, Catalepsie, Apoplexy, dead-Palsy, Coma, Falling-sickness, Convulsions, Cramps, Madness, Melancholy, Trembling.

2. Under TAURUS are all diseases incident to the Throat, as Kings evil, Quinsie, sore-Throat, Wens in the neck, Flux or rheum in the Throat.

3. Diseases under GEMINI are all such as are incident to the hands, arms and shoulders, whether they come really, or by accident, as fractures, dislocations, and such as come by blood-letting, corruption of the blood, windinesse in the blood, and indeed I have often found by experience, than GEMINI signifieth wind in the blood more than any other sign. I have now done with GEMINI, after I have told you my own opinion, which is, that the upper part of the shoulders, namely, that with which we carry burdens, is under TAURUS, which is the Embleme of labour; and net under GEMINI, as the common received opinion is.

4. Under CANCER are all Imperfections of the breast, stomack, Or liver whatsoever, as also whatsoever are incident to the breasts of women, as Cancer's there, and that inflammation which women commonly call the Ague in the breast; plurisies, want of appetite to victuals, want of digestion of victuals, coldness and over-heat of the stomack, dropsies, coughs; you may finde out the rest yourselves; the rule is as plain as the nose in a man's face.

5. Under LEO are all passions of the heart, as convulsions, saith my Author.

But if I may make so bold as to digress a little, I shall tell you, and prove it too when I am done, that convulsions are not a disease of the heart, but of the brain.

The truth is, it is one of old ARISTOTLE's opinions, which
crept into this noddle, as he was marring PLATO'S
Philosophy; the Nerves have their original from the brain;
convulsion is a plucking or twitching of the Nerves, Ergo, it
is a disease of the brain, not of the heart.

But to return to my purpose, under all
diseases the heart or back is subject to, as qualms
and passions, palpitation and trembling of the
heart, violent burning Feavers, sore eyes, the
yellow jaundice, and all diseases of choler, and
such diseases come of adjustion of blood, as the
Pestilence; and I am afraid LONDON will find this
too true so soon as SATURN comes into LEO. I pray
God mitigate this evil influence toward them at
that time.

6. Under VIRGO are all diseases incident to the bowels, the
meseraick veins, the Omentum, the diaphragm, spleen.
Take a few instances in this particular; worms, winde in the
guts, obstructions, the cholick and Iliak passions, hardness
of the Spleen, Hypochondriack melancholy.

7. Under LIBRA are diseases of the reins or kidneys, which
you please, for the significations of the words are the same;
heat of the reins in women, which sometimes causeth death
in travail, many times abortion, always hard labour, the
stone or gravel in the reins. And now let me teach you a
little; if MARS be significator of the disease, and in VIRGO,
it is the wind-cholick, without appearance either of gravel or
stone.

Have a care of your Patient, lest it turn to gravel in the
kidneys when he comes into LIBRA, and to the stone of the
bladder when he comes into SCORPION.

By your own ingenuity, if you have had any, you may by
this example find out twenty more like it.

Lastly, under LIBRA are all diseases coming of wind and
corruptions of blood.

8. Under the SCORPION are gravel and stone in
the bladder, inflammations and ulcers there; all

difficulties of urine whatsoever; all imperfections
of the urine, ruptures, fistulas, haemorroids,
the french pox, running of the reins, prispisnis; all diseases
that infect the privities of men or women.

All diseases of the womb, of which more in my
Guide for women, already in print.

9. Under SAGITTARIUS are all diseases in the thighs and
hips, as the Sciatica, &c. fistulas in those places, heat of
blood, pestilential feavers; and take this for a general rule,
that LEO and SAGITTARIUS signifie falls from horses, and
hurts by four-footed beasts, they being both of them signs of
horsemanship; besides SAGITTARIUS prejudith the body
by choier, heat, fire, and intemperance in sports.

10. Under CAPRICORN are all diseases in the knees and
hams; as paines, sprains, fractures, and dislocations:
leprosies, itch, scabs, all diseases of melancholy, and all
rumours called Schirrus.

11. Under AQUARIUS are all diseases incident to the legs
and ankles; all melancholy coagulated in the blood, cramps;
and the truth is, thickness of blood most usually proceeds
from this sign. Ask old SATURN, and he will tell you the
reason. By this the ingenuous have a plain way to find out
more; and by this Dr. Experience got materials to work with.

12. Under PISCES is all lamenesse, aches and diseases
incident to the feet; as Gouts, Kibes, Child-blains, &c. All
diseases coming of salt flegm, mixt humours, scabs, itch,
botches, and breaking out about the body, the small pox
and measles; all cold and moist diseases, and such as come
by catching wet and cold at the feet.

And if you will be pleased but to consider the
affinity PISCES holds with ARIES, you will soon see a
reason why wet taken at the feet strikes so speedily up to
the head.

As for Houses of the Heavens, they have the same
significations with the signs; the first House with ARIES, the
second with TAURUS, and so Analogically till you come to

the twelfth House, which bath the same signification that PISCES hath.

I have now done with this Part; only be pleased to notice that the fiery signes stir up diseases of choler, airy signes diseases of flegm, signs of double bodies diseases of mixt humours.

And thus much for this part, the pains of which have been mine, the benefit shall be yours, if you will but turn idleness out of doors, and place ingenuity in his room.

PART 111.
The Particular Parts and Members of the body which the Planets generally rule.

Herein I must either a little be critical, or else part from my loving friend Dr. Reason; I am loth to do the latter, and therefore must make bold with the former.

1. SATURNE, say Authors, rules in the body of man the spleen, and there he keeps his Court: The right Ear, the Bladder, the Bones, the Teeth, the retentive faculties throughout the body, which, what it is, be pleased to see my short Treatise of Human Vertues, in the latter end of my Ephemerides for Anno 1651, where you shall find not only what it is, but also what it is good for.

Against all this I except but against only one, which is the Bladder, for that is under the dominion of the Moon.

2. They say JUPITER rules the lungs, ribs, sides, liver, veins, blood, the digestive faculty, the natural-vertue of man which he rules, as Lawyers call it, TOTO ET IN SOLIDO.

Besides, Authors say he rules the arteries and seed; but how can they bring it about, I know not, nor I think themselves neither: why should JUPITER rule the arteries, when the Sun rules the heart ?

He that can give reason, ERIT MINI MAGNUS APPOLLO; and as little reason can be given, and that's little enough, why JUPITER should rule the seed, which is dame VENUS her fee-simple; surely the Planets will not rob one another, though men do; howsoever JUPITER seems to keep his court in the liver; and if you are minded to strengthen his operations in your bodies, begin there.

3. MARS rules in the body of men the gall, the Reins, the Veins, the Secrets, the left Ear; thus Authors; And there is but two true words in it, which is the gall and the left Ear. The truth is, he rules the apprehension, and that's the reason that cholerick men are so quick-witted.

Yes, a man of mean apprehension, when he is angry, will make a quicker apprehension in things satisfying his fury, then a man of quicker apprehension hath when he is pleased. Anger summons up all the powers of the body and mind to revenge wrong, though it be but imaginary. And then again, MARS rules that faculty which incites men to valour; he makes a man a Soldier every inch of him; he fortifies the smell, and that's the reason why Martial creatures have so good smell, as dogs, &c.

But very little reason, or none at all, unlesse you will make a reason of Tradition, who derives his degree rather from Dr. Corruption, then Doctor Reason, why MARS should rule the veins, seeing JUPITER rules the liver: If JUPITER rule the fountain, small he be deni'd the streams ? and then the Reins and Secrets are under VENUS, and that's apparent without any more dispute of the story.

4. VENUS rules the womb, testicles, yard and all the instruments of generation, the reins or the kidneys, the throat, womens breats, and milk, contained within them, the seed and liver.

But by my Author's favour, I can give no other reason why VENUS should rule the Liver, unlesse I should give this for a reason, because JUPITER stole the seed from her before; she to quit scores with him, steales away the liver from him.

Under the Dominion of MERCURY is the Brain, especially the rational part of it, the imagination, the tongue, hands and feet, the motional part of man. And that's the reason MERCURIALISTS (if MERCURY be strong) are so swift in motions, so fluent of speech.

He gives a quick apprehension, a strong imagination, and conceited; he makes a good Penman, and stirs up that faculty in man which causeth a thirst after knowledge; he is very fickle in his disposition, and that's that makes men so fickle-headed.

If SATURNE vouchsafe him a friendly look, ire is very constant; otherwise, if you look upon a Weather-cock, you may safely draw his picture, and no disparagement to his person either.

6. The SUN governs (if you will believe Authors) the brain and nerves, the heart and arteries, the sight, the eyes, the right eye of a man, the left eye of a woman' Against these I except, against the brain and nerves, the bulk of which is under the Moon.

Their operation is under MERCURY; now then if MERCURY afflict the brain, the failing is in the operation. If the Moon, in the bulk or body of the brain or nerves, he that is a Physician knows what the operations of Nature are: and then he knows what I say is truth, and the foundation of it built upon a Rock. He will esteem it as a Jewel.

It is the property of a fool to carp at what he cannot imitate.

7. Under the MOON is the bulk of the brain, the stomach, the bowels, the bladder, the taste, the left eye of a man, the right eye of a woman; a team of horses cannot draw me to believe that the MOON rules the taste.

If you please to peruse my Treatise of humane virtues, at the latter end of my Ephemeris for ANNO 1651. I think that you shall finde there that JUPITER. rules it: And my reason for it may there be found. Besides I have something from Dr. Experience for it, my own taste being exceeding good, and yet the MOON exceeding weak in my Genesis;

Being in a Cadent house and in Gemini, a sign which in my opinion more afflicts the MOON then CAPRICORNE.

I confess Mr. LILLY affirms GEMINI to be a most
noble signe, but I dare scarce believe him. ARIES is the most
principal of all the signes; GEMINI is cadent from ARIES.
ERGO, &c. But not now to enter into a contest with that
famous man, to whom this Nation is so much beholding.
Be pleased to take notice, that the twelfth house is more
inimical to the ascendant then the seventh; which if so, then
is the MOON more afflicted in GEMINI then in
CAPRICORNE.

PART IV.

*The particular parts of the body, under the several signes of the
Zodiac, and the houses in the heavens in a Celestial Scheme.*

1. Under ARIES is the head, and whatever belongs
to it, as its bones, the face, brain, hair, beard, eyes, nose,
tongue, &c. whatsoever in man is above the first Vertebra of
the neck.

2. Under Taurus is the neck, throat, the Vertebrae of the
neck, which are in number seven. The chanel-bone, the
shoulder blade, accoring to my opinion.
Also TAURUS hath again signification in the voice; for he
will roar like a Bull.

3. Under GEMINI are the shoulders, shoulder-bones, arms,
hands, fingers, together with their bag and baggage.

4. Under CANCER is the breast, ribs, lungs, pleura, the
ventricle of the stomack, womens breasts, the Liver, spleen,
&c. and yet Dr. Reason told me the other night that the
spleen was under VIRGO.

5. Under LEO is the heart, the back, and the Vertebrae of
the breast, which are in number twelve; the Pericardium;
some Authors say, the stomack is under LEO, but I can
scarce believe it: I am perswaded the appetite is under LEO,
and that's the reason such as have that signe ascending in
their Genesis are such greedy eaters.

You that are Astrologers, and have the Nativity of
such persons in your hands, you know my words are truth.

And if in a Nativity the prevalency of other significators should happen to contradict it.
You know the old Proverb, ONE SWALLOW MAKES NOT A SUMMER.
6. Under VIRGO is the belly and the bowels, the navel and spleen, the omentum, and all their appurtenances, &c.
    This is what she rules; and she bids you by my Pen to be chaste.
7. Under the Ballance, say Authors, are the reines, loyns, kidneys, between which (in my judgement) is as much difference as is between eight pence and two groats. Under LIBRA besides, they say, are the hams, buttocks, bladder and navel: Thus Authors. And I quoted only to this end, That young Students may see what a Monster Tradition is, and may avoid being led by the nose by it, as Beares are led to the stake. You know well enough, if the blind lead the blind, what will become of them both: Let every one, that desires to be called by the name of Artist, have his wits in his Head (for that's the place ordained for them) and not in his books.
    The hams are under CAPRICORNE, the bladder under SCORPIO, the navel under VIRGO; ask Doctor Reason, and see if he tell you not the same tale.
8. Under SCORPIO are the secrets of both sexes; it is not very fitting for me to name them; as also the Feminal vessels dedicated to the generation of man, the bladder and fundament; And therefore though Artists cry out so much against the SCORPION for a false, deceitful, treacherous, mischievous, violent, poysonsome sign; let them look back to the Rock from whence they are hewn; It may be that they shall see the reasons of some of their violent speeches against my self. A word is enough to wise men. Let them not speak evil of what they know not.
    This is most certain, from those parts of the body under the dominion of SCORPIO, have all men and women in general the influence of their propagation.

And in them take their greatest pleasure; and this have I spoken something for a Signe which every one speaks against.

9. Time will not stay therefore I must be brief; under SAGITTARIUS are the thighes, the bonecalled OS SACRUM, which whether justly so called or unjustly, I know not. It is either Jewish superstition or worse. The Rump-bone, the Thigh-bone, together with all the appurtances belonging to the thigh.

Some Authors say the hams are under SAGITTARIUS, but then they are beside the Cushion.

10. Under CAPRICORNE are the knees, hams, and what belongs unto them.

11. Under AQUARIUS are the legs and whatsoever belongs unto them, even from the outward skin called CUTICULA, to the midst of the marrow in both bones; For there are two of them, which Chirugians because they would keep you in ignorance, called FOCILE MAJUS & FOCILE MINUS, or if you will, TIBIA & FIBIA. They all know what the bones are but a quarter of them are not able to give you a reason why the bones are so called. Pray take notice of this, in going about to make slaves of you, they have made fools of themselves.

12. Lastly, PISCES claims the feet and ancles, toes and all the bones. To write like a scholler, 'tis TARSUS METATARSUS, and the bones of the toes. It rules also the skin of the foot, the flesh and vessels betwixt the skin and the bones.

Also some Authors hold an opinion that the signs carry the same signification in order that the houses of heaven do, and that ARIES should signifie life; TAURUS estate; GEMINI brethern and short journeys, you know the rest. Truly my own opinion is, many Authors invented whimsies, and when they had done, set them down to posterity for truth; who taking them up without tryal, cloathed Tradition in Plush and left poor Reason to go in Rags. An Author said so; ERGO, 'tis true, right or wrong.

I take this to be one of that generation, and I prove it thus: By this account CANCER should rule the Fathers, but experience tells us, that an ill Planet in CANCER in the GENESIS threatens evil to the Mother, but in LEO to the Father. A word is enough to a wise man.

Also there is another signification of the Planets, according to the respective signs they are in, every Planet making his own ARIES in his own house. I forbear here: First of all, because it conduceth not much to my present Scope: For Example, a Urine came to me about a year ago, Mercury was the afflicting Planet, and in ARIES; according to this rate, MERCURY rules the legs and privities; but the man was diseased in his head, for he was mad.

I gave you a Table of it in my GUIDE FOR WOMEN; and I am as loth to write one thing twice, as you are to pay for one thing twice. If this will not content you, you are so hard to be pleased, that I shall not undertake to please you, but to please my self; and in so doing I am confident to please some body else.

Chapter XI.
How the nature and kind of the disease may be found out by the figure of the Decumbiture.

1. The nature of the disease is to be found out three wayes: First by the Houses of heaven; of which, the sixth, seventh, & twelfth, signifie diseases.

2. By the nature of the signs, of which fiery signs signifie choler, and diseases thence proceeding; earthly signs signifie the diseases of melancholy; aery signes diseases of blood and wind; watry signes diseases of watry and salt flegm.

3. By the Planets themselves, and their Aspects; All this I shall make clear by this subsequent discourse, before which I shall premise these following Aphorisms: I. If SATURNE signifie the disease, 'tis like to continue long enough, if not too long: yet if he be with benevolents, it

mitigates; if with malevolents, it increaseth the evil. 2.
SATURNE in LEO or CAPRICORNE, with the Dragons
head or tail, or with VENUS combust, or with violent fixed
stars, he stirs up pestilences, or other pernicious feavers that
are little better.
3.Saturne alone in fiery signs shews hectick feavers.
4. In watry signs, sicknesses, or watry humours. The disease
comes of gross and vicious humours, a which will continue
long, with continual fluxes, and cold tremblings.
5. SATURN in moveable signes shewes flux of humours in
all parts of the body: Imagine the Dropsie, or other diseases
like it; and yet it is some question to me, whether SATURNE
causes Dropsies yea or no, unless afflicted by the MOON in
signification.
6. SATURNE in common signs gives compound diseases,
and such as run out of one disease into another, and yet
they pass leisurely out of one disease into another; you may
almost whip a snail as fast, you may easily see it before it
come if your eyes be in your head.
7. SATURNE in fixed signs, if in LEO gives hectique feavers,
in other fixed signs quartain agues, goyts) leprosies, and
other diseases that stay longer then they are welcome.
8. If JUPITER cause the disease, look to the liver, for thats
afflicted, the digestion is bad; blood abounds either in
quantity or in quality; a thousand to one if it be not too hot.
9. JUPITER in fiery signs bestows men such feavers as come
of blood without putrefaction, such as the Greeks call
SYNOCHUS NON PUTRIDA, they last but a very little
while.
10. MARS gives violent feavers with putrefacti.ons, and the
SUN gives no other.
11. If you find MARS in a fiery sign, judge the disease either
a burning feaver, or else the pestilence; if SATURNE bear a
share in signification with him, melancholy bears a share, or
else ajudge choler, which is more usual.
12. MARS in common signs varies the diseases, take heed of
a relapse; the Crisis is as certain as a Weather-cock; so

exceeding swift and sudden will they come, even as swift as the Wind, not waiting the MOON's leisure: In such a case you may more safely judge by the aspects of the MOON to the Planets then by the Crisis.

13. MARS in LEO afflicts the heart, the disease is a feaver, and the cause of it choler.

14. Always when MARS signifies the disease it is very short but extream acute.

15. If the SUN at the decumbiture be afflicted by the body or quartile, opposition, Antiscion of SATURNE, the disease is SATURNINE melancholy, and will in all probability last longer then you would willingly have it.

16. If the SUN be afflicted in the same manner by MARS, the cause is choler; the motion of the disease is as swift as the wind, and as violent as the Whirlwind.

17. If VENUS be ill-affected to the sick, the disease comes of intemperance; either one way or other; Perhaps with drinking, perhaps by venereal sports; what e're the cause be, those parts of the body signified by VENUS suffer for it.

18. VENUS in fiery signs causeth one day Feavers; but if MARS joyn with her in signification, the Feaver is rotten and proceeds from flegme.

19. If MERCURY be infortunate and cause the disease, he proclaims that the infirmity lies in the brain, perhaps madness, or falling sickness, or it may be the man dreams waking.

20. If MERCURY joyn in signification with MARS, you may be confident the disease is a frenzy.

21. The Lord of the ninth in the sixth, Witchcraft is to be feared, or else the disease lies very occult; I doubt my Author is mistaken: Surely it should be the Lord of the twelfth in the sixth; for the Lord of the ninth should rather occasion the disease about some whimsies in Religion.

The MOON in ARIES in the eighth afflicts the head with a disease too hot for it to beare whether the disease lie in the mind or in the body.

Chapter XII.

How to know whether the disease be in the minde, or in the body.

All the Aphorisms of my Author upon this question, are got so deeply together by the ears, and in such a hubbub, that I know not in the world which way to go about to reconcile them; every following Aphorism thwarts him that goes before; in one he affirms that the SUN, MOON and Ascendant rule the body, and their Lords the minde: The very next Aphorism affirms the contrary; most of them contradict one another in such a hideous manner, that I was forced to leave their companies, and search other Authors for a Resolution of this point; and they conclude, that the SUN, MOON and Ascendant signifies the body, and their Lords the mind, and if this may be taken for truth, the directed Aphorisms are these:

1. The SUN, MOON, and Lord of the ascendant impedited, and their Lords safe, sheaves the disease lies in the body and not in the minde.

2. If their Lords be impedited, and they safe, the disease lies in the minde, and not in the body.

3. If both SUN and MOON and the Ascendant and their Lords also be impedited, or the greatest part of them, both body and mind are diseased; and this I confesse is something rational.

4. SATURNE generally signifies of melancholy, and by consequence alienation of minde, madnesse, &c. and there fore alwayes when you find him to be signficator of the disease, or in the ascendant, or in the sixth House afflicting the Lord of the ascendant, or either of the Luminaries, the sick is afflicted with care, or grief, or something else that's as bad; be sure the mind suffers for it.

5. If JUPITER be significator of the disease, it lies in the body, if it lies anywhere; for JUPITER never troubles the minde, unlesse it be that Monster which men call Religion.

6. It were a good thing when a man is troubled in minde, if an Artist could tell the cause of this his trouble; that you may do so, make use of these two or three rules; there is

enough of them, though there be but few; if you have but
wit enough to know by a penny how a shilling is coyned,
they are these;

1. If the SUN be author of the distemper, as he may be, if he
be Lord of the Ascendant, sixth or twelfth house, the
distemper comes through pride, ambition, vain-glory.

2. If it be JUPITER, it comes through religion, some idle
Priest hath fear'd the poor creature out of his wits.

3. If it be VENUS, love, luxurious expence, or something else
of like nature is the cause.

4. If MERCURY be the afflicting Planet, the sick is pestered
with a parcel of strange imaginations, and as many vain
fears attend him; great vexation, or study, or both is the
cause.

5. SATURNE, Jealousie, fear, &c.

6. MARS, Through anger, contention, violent passion, &c.

7. MOON, Care, fear, drunkenness, &c.

By these you may find out all the rest, for this is the sum of
the business.

Chapter XIII.

How it may be known what part of the body is afflicted.

That this may be known, for 'tis not only possible, but also
probable, be pleased to consider.

1. If the sign of the Lord of the sixth possesseth, especially if
he be an infortune, or a fortune infortunated. And then

2. Consider what part of the body the sign he is in governs,
as ARIES governs the head, TAURUS the neck and throat,
&c. and be sure that part is afflicted ....

3. Consider what parts of the body the afflicting Planet
rules, [Viz. the Planet that afflicts the sixth or planet there]
what sign, which are under that sign, and you need not
question but that's afflicted; for example, VENUS though
she rules many parts of the body, yet in SCORPIO she rules
onely the privities.

4. SATURNE Lord of the sixth and in the tenth, in TAURUS
afflicts the body universally, but especially the left side.

5. SATURN Lord of the sixth in the last degree of GEMINI, or in the first degree of CANCER, causeth pain in the left side, as though an awl were run into it.

6. SATURN Lord of the sixth in LEO in the second liouse, causeth pains in the back and heart, the original of which (saith my Author) is blood; but I should rather think it Melancholy.

7. If he be in VIRGO in the twelfth house, signifies pain in the head; if he be in SCORPIO oriental and slow in motion, signifies diseases in the reigns, as the gravel, stone and pissing blood. I confess I can give no reason for all this.

8. If SATURN be Lord of the disease and in AQUARIUS, the disease comes by travel.

9. MARS Lord of the sixth and in the fifth, and in SCORPIO gives an internal pain in all parts of the body; If it be a woman she is not well in her Wombe, the illness of which afflicts all her body, especially her head, by reason of that admirable congruity betwixt that part and her Womb; kind women take notice of it; For it is as true as that the SUN is up when he is upon the meridian. All Cephalick medicines help the Womb and remedy its grief; I am confident you desire a reason of it; You shall not fail of your desires. It is because ARIES and SCORPIO are both the houses of MARS. (And so in all aspects in physical judgment to consider the part the Aspecting Planet governs in that sign he aspects, as if any planets Aspect the Aged, see whether the Planet Aspecting governs first in that sign, so that part is afflicted according to the nature of the planet afflicing.

You may if you please consider according to the 2d rule what sign the planet afflicting is in.)

10. If MARS be retrograde in SCORPIO and in the Ascendant, the whole body is universally afflicted, but externally, VIZ. the man breaks out in boils and ulcers, perhaps it is the gmall pox or measles; if VENUS set forward the mischief, the French pox is shrewdly to be suspected.

11. If MARS be Lord of the sixth in LEO, the sick is extreamly pained in his back; in this you need never fear failing.

12. If MARS be Lord of the sixth in VIRGO, my Author saith it will lie in the left side, or left legge; But after I had had half an hours talk with Doctor Experience, he proved to me it was always the Cholick, and heat in the bowels, take heed it comes not to the gravel in the kidneys, when MARS comes into LIBRA, and to the stone in the bladder, when MARS comes to SCORPIO. He that is a Physitian, knowes as well how to prevent a diseases before it comes, as how to remedy it when it is come.

13. The MOON in the Ascendant afflicted by Saturn or MARS, bestows difficulty breathing, and infirmities in the lungs upon a man; I confess I can give no reason for it.

14. VENUS Lady of the sixth and infortunated by MARS, gives suspitions enough of the French pox.

      Here is enough to teach you more; let not all your wits lye in your books; be diligent and studious, or else you may happen to dye fools; let not all your wits lye in your books, but some in your head; it is that within you, and not that without you must do you good.

As for the side of the body afflicted, my Author hath left a few Rules to know it, which I will declare to you, and leave them to the approbation or exprobation of Doctor Experience; they are these:

1. If the Lord of the sixth be afflicted above the earth, and in a diurnal sign, the sickness is in the right side of the body, and in the upper part of it.

2. If the Lord of the sixth be under the earth, and in a nocturnal sign, the sickness lyes in the inferiour parts of the body, and on the left side.

3. Whether he be under or above the earth in a diurnal, the sickness is in the forepart of the body, imagine the forehead, face, breast, belly, or some other visible part.

4. If it be in a noctural sign, the disease lyes in the back part of the body, or else in some part that lyes invisible, as the

bowels; &c or perhaps the disease lyes occult; for take this
for a general rule, the diseases are more hid from the eyes of
your understanding, when the significators of them are in
nocturnal signs, then they are when they are in diurnal.
5. If the significators are corrupted by other Planets, and a
difference in these rules between the significators and the
Planet that corrupts them, the Patient is afflicted bothways;
namely according as he signifies, and according as the
Planet corrupting signifies.
6. In such a case view diligently which of them is most
afflicted: And your reason, if you have any, will tell you that
the most part of the malady lyes in that part of the body
signified by the Planet which is most afflicted.
7. To wind up all in a word, Masculine Planets denote the
right side of the body, Feminine the left, all of them afflict
that part of the body which they govern, as VENUS secrets,
Mars head, &c.

Chapter XIV.
*Whether the Disease shall be long or short, or whether it shall end
in Life or Death.*

For judging of this, take a few cautions by the way.
1. Consider if the SUN, MOON and Ascendant and their
Lords be much or little afflicted.
2. Consider the age of the sick party; for old age brings
longer sickness then youth.
3. Consider the time of year; for Autumn and Winter bring
longer sicknesses then Spring and Summer.
4. Consider the complexion of the Patient; for a melancholy
man is more subject to retain a sickness then a cholerick.
5. Consider the Planet afflicting, for SATURNE produceth
longer sickness then MARS.
6. The Planets generally and briefly order the sicknesses
they give in this manner; SATURNE gives long sicknesses;
the SUN and JUPITER short, MARS shorter then either of
them, but acute; VENUS mean, MERCURY various and
unconstant, according to the Planet he is joined with or

aspected to The MOON gives such sickness as often returns, as Agues, falling sicknesse, &c. And therefore the direction of the MOON to the body, or aspect of SATURN will sooner cause a falling-sicknesse then the direction of any other significator.

These are the cautions, and according to these cautions so understand these following Aphorisms which you shall find marshalled into three divisions; First, Signes of long or short sicknesses Second, Signes of recovery; Thirdly, Signes of death.

PART 1.
Signes of long or short sicknesse.

First, the sixth house being possessed by a fixed sign, argues length in the disease; if the signe that possesseth the Cuspe of the sixth be moveable, the disease will be short; if the sign be common, the disease will either be mean in respect of length, or else a change of the disease, or a relapse is to be feared.

2. If the latter degrees of a signe be upon the Cuspe of the sixth, the disease will quickly end either one way or another.

3. A fixed signe on the Cuspe of the sixth, shewes tough and hard humours to be causes of the disease, and such as are hard to be expelled, they stick to the body like birdlime.

4. SATURN Lord of the sixth shewes long diseases; JUPITER, MARS and the SUN short; MERCURY such as are as constant as the weathercock.

5. If the Lord of the sixth be stronger than the Lord of the Ascendant, the sickness gets strength against nature; if you find it is so upon a figure in urine, judge the disease increaseth.

6. If the Lord of the sixth be weaker then the Lord of the Ascendant, nature gets strength over the disease, and will at last put him to a total rout.

7. Common signes shew the disease will stay in one state, as long as a Cat is tyed to a Pudding.

8. The Lord of the sixth, if he be a malevolent it is an ill omen; if it be a benevolent, you need not so much as fear a long sicknesse, for the disease will be cured both speedily and easily; unless the said benevolent be Lord also of the eighth.

9. If the MOON apply to the Lord of the sixth, the disease will be encreased till it has put life to its trumps.

If the MOON be Lady of the Ascendant, ill dyet was the cause of it; perhaps a surfeit of drinking.

If VENUS be Lady of the sixth, 'tis women, or it may be sports and pastimes, or such gewgaws as VENUS delights in; you know how to judge the rest of the Planets according to their several natures.

10. If the Lord of the sixth apply to the Quartile or Opposition of the Lord of the Ascendant, the disease encreaseth, and is not yet come to his height.

I confesse this and many other Aphorisms hereabouts, belong not at all to the decumbiture, but to question upon Urine, and most of them, if not all of them, will hold true in them also.

11. The Lord of the sixth in the eighth is but a scurvy unlucky sign, and shewes the sicknesse will end in death: if it be in the fourth, it shewes the sicknesse will end in the grave.

12. The Lord of the sixth in the twelfth, cryes aloud that the Patient opposeth his own health.

13. The Lord of the eighth in the sixth, and the Lord of the sixth in the eighth, if they be in friendly aspect, the sick soon recovers.

14. I confesse the former Aphorisme seems a Paradox to me; I should rather think sicknesse and death had made a match together, to take away the life of the patient, and shall do so still, till I have spoken with Doctor Experience about it.

15. If there be an Opposition, Sextile, or Trine between the Lord of the sixth and JUPITER, the sick soon recovers; for JUPITER will handle him without mittons, and 'tis very

probable VENUS will not come much behind them in the businesse.

I doubt my Author mistook the ninth house for the tenth; did I say doubted it ? nay, I know it.

17. A malevolent in the sixth, is an ill signer but a benevolent there is as good as one for all that.

18. The Lord of the twelfth in the sixth shewes Witchcraft or possession by the Devil, that's bad; and if he be a malevolent, you may take it for granted, 'tis as sure as a club.

19. The Lord of the Ascendant in the sixth and the Lord of the sixth in the Ascendant, shewes long diseases, and such as will continue till one of them, if not till both of them make his exit out of the sign he is in.

20. If in such a case the malevolent cast ill aspects to her, bid her Physitian use his wits as far as he can, for the fear of death is not small.

21. The Lord of the Ascendant and sixth house, in Quartile, Opposition, or Conjunction, in such degrees as Artists call CAZEMINI, and in Angles, threatens such perpetual pain, which none but Doctor death is likely to cure.

22. The Lord of the sixth in the Ascendant shewes the disease will continue long enough, nay longer then 'tis welcome; but it doth not signifie the sick needs dye; for that belongs to the eighth house and its Lord.

23. 'tis no good sign of quick recovery, when the lord of the sixth house is malevolent.

24. If the SUN, MOON and Lord of the Ascendant be free from ill beames of ill Planets; and apply to fortunes that are any thing strong and like to do good, the cure will come as soon as you can in reason hope for it.

25. 'Tis always bad when the SUN, MOON, or Lord of the Ascendant apply to the Lord of the sixth, eighth, or twelfth houses; and 'tis not a whit better, if they be Lords of those houses.

26. It is an exceeding good signe at the beginning of a sicknesse, if neither the Lord of the Ascendant, SUN or MOON behold the Lord of the sixth or eighth house.

27. Its very ill when the Lord of the Ascendant is afflicted, namely if he be retrograde or in an ill house, in his detriment or fall, or beseiged by malevolents. All houses which behold not the Ascendants are ill houses; namely the sixth, eighth, and twelfth: I will take no notice at all of the second in this case because it is succeeding to the first; but the seventh shall not escape so, because it opposeth the Ascendants; it is very bad when the Lord of the Ascendant is there.

28. In such cases 'tis true the disease may be happily cured, if good courses be taken; but either a relapse into that disease is to be feared, or else the disease is subject to a change out of that disease into another as bad, whereby the sick is in danger of death, unlesse in the mean season the Lord of the Ascendant growes stronger; for the stronger he is, the better able he is to preserve life.

29. The Lord of the Ascendant infortunated by the Lord of the sixth, though he be but in his terme, prolongs the sicknesse.

30. If the Lord of the Ascendant be infortunated by the Lord of the eighth, it gives fear enough, that none but death can end the quarrel between the sick and the sicknesse.

31. If the Lord of the Ascendant be slow in motion, the sicknesse will as slow in the parting, and slower if SATURN be Lord of the Ascendant; but if the Lord of the Ascendant be swift in motion, according to the haste he makes such speed you may expect of the disease.

32. The Lord of the Ascendant angular and strong, and no way impeded, let the disease be never so violent, the feare of death is more than the harme.

33. The Lord of the Ascendant entering into another signe, though it be out of his own house into another, provided it be not into the house of the Lord of the sixth, eighth or twelfth, the disease soon ends in health; if it be into the house of the Lord of the eighth, the sick dyes at the time; if it be into the house of the Lord of the sixth, the sicknesse is encreased; if into the house of the Lord of the twelfth, the

sick either keeps ill diet, or is unruly, or is mad; in such a case he that will not be ruled by reason, must be ruled by force.

34. If the Lord of the Ascendant be weake of himself, yet if he be joyned to a fortune, the recovery will be very speedily; for if the fortune be anything strong, he will helpe it forward with tooth and mile.

35. The Lord of the Ascendant, the SUN or MOON joyned to an infortune, prolongs the disease; and the weaker they are, the longer is the disease like to last.

36. If the significator of the disease be in a signe of the nature of the disease. for example, suppose the disease proceeds of melancholy, if the significator be in an earthly sign, it exceedingly prolongs the disease; judge the like by the rest of the humours, in such cases the cure is exceedingly difficult: VIS UNITA FORTIER.

37. IF the significator of the sicknesse be an infortune, and applied to the Lord of the Ascendant, it mightily retards the cure; you see what need there is the Physitian be an Astrologer; I know not how a man should help nature unlesse he know it.

38. If the MOON be with the Lord of the Ascendant, or applyed to him, the cure comes gallantly on, if she be swift in motion; but if she be slow in motion, she hales the cure backwards.

39. If the MOON decrease both in light and motion, and be with the Quartile, Opposition, or body of SATURNE, the disease is extreame; for the next time she comes to his body or opposition, unlesse you cure the disease before, and he is a Physitian indeed that can doe it, death takes possession of the breathlesse Corps of the Patient.

40. The MOON, or any other significator of the sick joyned to a Planet direct and swift in motion, shewes but a short sicknesses But if the Planet be retrograde or slow, the cure will be as slow to a hair.

41. If SCORPION ascend, the sick is the causer of his own sicknesse, because then ARIES is upon the Cuspe of the

sixth house, and one Planet is Lord of both places; and if he
be in either of both these houses, it is so much the worse, for
he will adde fire to the fuel, and blow the Bellowes too.
42. Both the Luminaries in Cadent houses and their
dispositors together with the Lord of the Ascendant
afflicted, show a disease so dangerous, that the Physitian
bath need enough to look about him.
43. If in such a case the benevolents set their helping hands,
the disease will be prolonged and for acute become
chronick; yet if the benevolent be strongest, the disease will
at last be cured beyond all hope; if the malevolents be
strongest, 'tis shrewdly to be feared that death must turn
Physitian when all comes to all.
44.Suppose MARS be Lord of the Ascendant, and in the
sixth, yet if he be in any aspect to VENUS, 'tis not
desperately bad, because she mitigates the evil.
45. The Lord of the sixth in the eighth afflicted by SATURN
or MARS, if he be weak, viz. retrograde or combust, or in his
detriment, the disease will continue till death cures it.
46. The SUN, MOON, or Lord of the Ascendant with a
fortune, and that fortune they are with retrograde,
promiseth cure; but together with the promise comes a
threatening of length of the disease.
47. The MOON in a bad place of the heavens prolongs the
disease if she be in a fixed signe, without any further
dispute of the story.
48. Never forget this general rule, the stronger the MOON is
at the Decumbiture, the better it is for the sick; the weaker
she is at that time, the worse.
49. It were a good thing and very commendable if the
nativity of the sick could be procured, for if SATURN be
Lord of the nativity, the sick may live though the MOON be
in conjunction with his body, or opposition at the
decumbiture.
50. Judge of the length or shortnesse of the disease
according as the disease is: for it is not to be expected that a

Feaver should last seven years; and it is as little to be hoped that a Consumption should be cured in a day.

PART II.
Signes of life at the Decumbiture.

First, JUPITER, VENUS, the SUN and M00N in the Ascendant, nor afflicting or beholding the Lord of the eighth themselves, take away not only fear of death, but also promise a speedy cure.

2. The conjunction of the MOON with JUPITER is always prosperous: most propitious if it be in CANCER: if doubtful at all, it is when they are in CAPRICORN, because in the one they are both dignified: in the other both Cadent from the dignities. And yet let me tell you but this much, JUPITER is JUPITER still, be he where he will.

3. The MOON in an angle well desposed in good terms, and free from the body or beames of SATURN or MARS, it restores sick to health, and scornes to be beholding to any of them all.

4. The MOON applying to the Lord of the Ascendant, unlesse she carries the beames of the Lord of death to him, doth the like.

5. The MOON increasing in light and swift in motion, and not posited in the sixth, eighth, nor twelfth houses, applying to the Sextile, Trine, or Antiscion of the Lord of the Ascendant, though the Lord of the Ascendant be a malevolent, it matters not, so he be direct, and not infortunated by house, nor impeded by another malevolent, neither in his detriment nor fall, it promiseth recovery.

6. If the MOON be void of course at the decumbiture, if on the Critical day she behold a good star, there is no question of recovery to be made.

7. If on a Critical day the MOON be in her own house, or exaltation, though she be void of course, the fear of death is more than the harm, for the sick will recover.

8. The SUN, MOON, and Lord of the Ascendant free from the beams of SATURN, MARS, or the Lord of death at the decumbiture, there can not be so much as a bare suspition of death.

9. If the benevolents be stronger then the malevolents at the decumbiture, and withall if they behold the MOON, the Ascendant, or his Lord, they they promise recovery. The Malevolents may threaten hard, &c. but the benevolents will stay the deadly blow.

10. If the MOON be separated from a weake malevolent, and applyed to a strong benevolent, the sick is easily recovered; for the weakest always goes to the wall.

11. If SATURN be significator of the sicknesse, oriental to the SUN, the disease coming of cold, &c., occidental of the SUN, the disease coming of heat, seldome kills: My Author may be something questioned for this; yet this I'le easily grant him, that SATURN is not so subject to take away life in such a case as in the contrary.

I dare not be positive in the things, because I have not spoken with Dr. Experience about it.

12. MARS is not so formidable when he is occidental as when he is oriental.

13. MARS afflicteth the MOON more when she is oriental then he doth when she is occidental.

14. A reception between the Lord of the Ascendant and the Lord of the eighth, if they be benevolent, or if the benevolent lend them aid, shewes recovery.

15. Also my Author saith, that if the Lord of the eighth receiveth the Lord of the Ascendant without the malicious beames of ill fortunes, the sick will escape, even when there is no hope of life.

I know not the truth of it, because as yet I know not the judgement of Doctor Experience in the thing; but Dr. Reason is of opinion, that it is far better that the Lord of the Ascendant dispose of the Lord of the 8th, then that the Lord of the 8th dispose of the Lord of the Ascendant.

Is it not better that life dispose of death then that death dispose of life ? Indeed this he told me, That if the Lord of the Ascendant do dispose the Lord of the 8th, the sick will take such a course as will be for his own prejudice, and the hastning on of his end.

But if sick people will not be ruled by fair means, -they must be ruled by foul; and that is all that I can say unto it.

16. If good Planets be in the Ascendant or Mid-heaven 'at the Decumbiture, and pretty strong withal, they will stand to their tackling stoutly to maintain life, though the significators of it be never so much afflicted.

PART III.

Signes of Death.

First of all the Lord of the Ascendant afflicted in the 8th; the Patient is more made to be APUD INFERNOS, then death is to have him; The man will dye, and his life will be cast away absolutely with evil guidance.

2. If at the Decumbiture you find the Lord of the Ascendant combust in the Ascendant, posse the same judgment with the former.

3. If the Lord of the 8th house be in the mid-heaven, and afflict the Lord of the Ascendant, the Physitian will be in a shrewd mistake, and instead of curing go near to kill. Listen to this, O Colledge of Physitians; let me intreat you to learn the principles of your trade; and I beseech you no longer mistake avarice for wit and honesty.

4. The Lord of the 8th very strong in the Ascendant, gives you fair warning that death is a coming.

5. A conjunction between the Lord of the 8th and the Lord of the Ascendant, is as moral a sign as the heavens can shew.

6. It is a very unlucky sign when the Lord of the 8th house is Lord of the house at the Decumbiture. And not much better if the Lord of the house at the Decumbiture be afflicted by the Lord of the 8th; especially if the Lord of the 8th be malevolent.

Such ill beginning of a disease usually proves fatal at the latter end, unless the Physitian be a very able man.

7. If the Lord of the Ascendant fall retrograde from the Body of the Lord of the 8th, it gives you a timely warning of death at their next conjunction, unless the Lord of the Ascendant meet with the SUN before he meet with the Lord of death again.

8. The Lord of the 8th in conjunction, square, or opposition to the MOON at the Decumbiture, threatens death unless there be a reception between them. If the Lord of the 8th be retrograde or infortunated, you may the more confide in his judgment.

9. The Lord of the eighth in an angle, especially the western angle, the MOON and Lord of the Ascendant being in cadent houses, or afflicted by malevolents, death may be feared, and that justly so especially if a malevolent be in the eighth, or Lord of that house.

10. The MOON with both SATURN and JUPITER, profits not the sick at all, unless JUPITER be much stronger than SATURN, or with the Lord of the Ascendant then either of them.

In such a case medicines under the influence of JUPITER will do good, because his body is afflicted by so potent an adversary.

This had I from Doctor Reason; neither is it barely to systeme truth, but a foundation to build other truths upon; a rule for practice; a key to open the closet of practice, an heuretes to find other truths by.

11. The Lord of the Ascendant in the aspects, or with the antiscion of an infortune in the eighth, threatens death unless the wholesome beams of JUPITER and VENUS help; which if, there will be a strong contest between nature and disease.

The fortunes strive to maintain nature, the infortunes to destroy him. In such case look which is the strongest, and pass judgment upon the end of the dispute accordingly.

12. If you find the MOON in like case in an acute disease, or the SUN in a Chronical, pass the same judgment.

If there be a reception between the Lord of the Ascendant and the Lord of the eighth by any aspect, the sick will probably live; and that as I remember, I told you before. But the sickness will be long and tedious, and the effects of it lye long in the body, and that I never told you till now.

14. The MOON with SATURN and MARS, or the MOON with the one, and the SUN with the other, or either of them with one, and the Lord of the Ascendant with the other, or the Lord of the Ascendant with both, gives shrewd suspitions, that the sickness is but the PROMODUS or usherer in of death.

15. The slower in motion the afflicting infortune is, the worse it is; for then the MOON meets him again upon the Critical day.

16. The Lord of the Ascendant in the seventh or fourth house, and there afflicted gives warning to the sick man that his dissolution is at hand.

17. An infortune upon the Cuspe of the Horoscope, bids the sick provide for a change.

18. Fixed stars of a violent nature, speak the same language, if they be upon the Horoscope.

19. Those fixed stars are said to be of a violent nature, which are of the nature of SATURN and MARS; as LANX AUSTRALIS, the BULS eyes, the SCORPION's heart, &c. and some which are of the nature of the fortunes, if Authors mistake not their natures, as ALGOL, or the head of the MEDUSA which is placed in the Buckler of Perseus. The Grecian Astrologers called him the Devils head; and yet all the Astrologers hold JUPITER and VENUS to have share in his nature. Let it suffice that all hold, and Doctor Experience himself certifies, that his conditions are as bad as who is worst. Neither shall he come behind any one of the fired stars in doing mi-schief.

22. Both the Luminaries afflicted under the earth, carry the same signification.

23. It is evil if the MOON be in her detriment or fall at the Crisis, though she be not afflicted at all; the time of the Crisis is the time of a combat between nature and the disease.

And if the MOON be weak, she is not able to maintain nature in the combat.

24. The SUN afflicted by the body, Square or Opposition ,or Antiscion of a malevolent, it tells the Patient the disease will be long and tedious if not mortal; and bids him provide himself with such a Physitian as knows how to do something else besides only to tell money.

25. The MOON opposed to the Lord of the Ascendant at the beginning of a sicknesse, if the Lord of the Ascendant be also retrograde or combust, shewes bitter accidents will fall out to the sick during the time of his sicknesses he is a wise Physitian that can remedy them; but he is wise that can anticipate them.

26. The MOON in the fourth house with the body square, opposition or antiscion of MARS, soon brings a man to his last inheritance, the grave; she threatens it, if she be there no way afflicted, unless she be very strong.

27. As I have judged by the MOON, so judge by MARS if you find him; for if he being there have any dignities in the Ascendant, he will urge a man so fast to his grave, as ever sleep urged him to bed.

SATURNE opposite to the Lord of the 8th house, threatens danger enough to the sick.

29. The MOON in conjunction with MARS in the fourth house will send the sick to take a supper in another world, though both their fortunes stand and look upon trim.

30. The MOON in the Ascendant, if you will believe Authors, always hurts; and they give some shew of reason of it, because there she hath most power over the body of the sick.

Yet mine own opinion for the present is, that if she be there, and in CANCER or TAURUS, she will rather help then hinder the sick. If the MOON do hate the Ascendant, as Authors say, I suppose the reason to be because SATURN loves it; and then she hates the 8th and 12th houses by the same Rule. And if you will call your wits into examination, they will tell you it is true enough.

31. If the MOON be in the Ascendant, and the sign ascending of a contrary nature to her, it is a hundred to one that the sick dye not of that disease.

And here my Author spoke something to the purpose; if the former Aphorism made a discord in your brain, this, if rightly understood, will reduce them to harmony.

32. The MOON applying to the body of the SUN within twelve degrees of the decumbiture, the sicknesse comes not so much to terrific your body, as to give you warning of your end.

And the nearer the MOON is to the body of the SUN, the speedier dispatch will death make of the body of his captive.

33. The MOON beseiged by the bodies of the malevolents posited between the SUN and one of them, the hopes of life are very small, or none at all.

34. Authors say, that if a man or woman fall sick when the MOON is going out of combustion, their sickness will encrease till she comes to the opposition of the SUN. And if then she meet with as ill Planet, the sick recovers if not they die. For mine own particular, I speak no more then I have found by continual experience; I have often found this false, and never true.

35. If the SUN and MOON be Lord of the house at the decumbiture, and behold the Lord of the eighth, the sicknesse is sent to proclaim the approach of death.

36. It is very bad when the MOON carries light of the Lord of the Ascendant to the Lord of the eighth, it threatens death, but it does not so in all diseases neither; For example, in such as come and goe by fits as Agues, Falling-sickness,

&c. you may make this use of it, that none are fit to make Physitians, but such as are intimately acquainted with Madame Nature, and her eldest son Dr. Reason.

37. It is extream bad when the MOON applies to any star in the eighth, as bad as when she applies to the Lord of the eighth hiniself.

38. The MOON combust in the eighth in LEO, threatens death, says my Author; and so the truth is she doth, if she be combust in any other house or sign, unlesse she separate from the body of the SUN.

39. The disease will appear little otherwise then the forerunner of death, if the MOON be in LIBRA, and JUPITER and VENUS in conjunction; he that knows any thing in Physick that he should know, knows the reason well enough.

40. The MOON with the Pleiades, and the Aldebaran, or with any other violent fixed star, shews danger of death.

41. The MOON applying to her own Nodes, namely the head and taile of the Dragon, is very bad, but not so bad if she separate from them.

42. It is very bad when SATURN is in his Perigaeon, or near it, if the disease come of retention.

43. Judge the like by MARS, if the disease be a Feaver, or proceed of choler; and here you have another instructor to teach you knowledge; the nearer a planet is to the earth, the more stoutly will he maintain and encrease the humours he governs.

44. It is a very bad sign, if not desperate, if there be an Eclipse of either Luminary upon a Critical day; and if it miss a day of it, it will break no squares in such a case; the time of the Eclipse bath to my knowledge anticipated the time of the Crisis a whole day natural, and proved mortal too, as I have had experience in Essex, in the latter end of October, 1649.

Chapter XV.
For the Cure of any disease, take these few Rules.

First see what the Disease is.

2. Consider who is the Author or Causer of it; and that you may see, if you consider what Planet governs that disease.

3. Consider whether it be caused by the Sympathy or Antipathy of the Planet.

4. And that you may know this (which is the whole key of Physick) Consider I. Whether the Planet afflicting do govern the part afflicted; and if he have any dominion in that part of the body, he causes it by Sympathy; one example all: As suppose diseases in the bones, Spleen, &c. if SATURN be the cause of it, it's by Sympathy, because he governs those parts.

5. If by Antipathy, consider what part of the body any Planet afflicts, either by his presence or aspects; and then secondly consider who or what Planet governs that part; if the Planet afflicting be an enemy to the Planet governing that part, then the disease is caused by Antipathy.

6. As is the disease, so is the cure.

7. If by Antipathy, then apply those medicines proper to the place affected and governed by the afflicted Planet; so here is cure by Antipathy,
as suppose Saturn afflicts some parts that the MOON governs, here the disease is cured by Antipathy because SATURN is an enemy to the MOON; to cure which, apply things proper to the part affected and governed by the MOON, because they are antipathetical to the disease caused by SATURN.

8. If the disease be caused by Sympathy, then you must apply medicaments to the part affected, or disease affecting, and governing by that Planet afflicting; here is cure by Sympathy, here the Planet that kills or strikes is repel'd, or is beat by his own weapons.

9. A Disease may be cured by Sympathy or Antipathy another way.

By Sympathy thus: When a Planet afflicts, or causes a disease, the cure may be made by applying medicaments to the part affected, or disease affecting (and that you must be sure always to observe) and governed by another Planet with the afflicting Planet.

By Antipathy MUTATIS MUTANDIS, &c. with this caution, use no Antipathetical medicines. These few Rules well observed may make a fool a Physitian.

10. By the foregoing rules it seems all or most of the Planets do govern some one or more particular things proper to all or most disease, by which it will follow that every Planet hath a share in every particular member there by Sympathy or Antipathy, as to the member itself, or Planet governing it.

12. I answer in general, every particular Planet has a compound or mixt share in every part, like as has the four Elements: But particularly every Planet has share in every part, either Sympathetically, or Antipathetically: Hereby you see without any Colledge-light,that one medicine may cure or be good for more diseases than one, and so may cure one disease by sympathy, another by Antipathy; that which may be a SATURNIAN disease by Sympathy (viz. when SATURN causes the disease, and afflicts any parts he himself governs) may cure a LUNARIAN disease by Antipathy, when the MOON afflicts any parts SATURN governs; so whereas the medicine cured when he caused the disease himself, so here it cures being caused by another, by Antipathy, because these things which SATURNE governes, are Antipathetical to the afflictions or diseases of the MOON or MOON causes.

HERMES TRISMEGISTUS
UPON THE FIRST DECUMBITURE OF THE SICK.

SHEWING THE SIGNS AND CONJECTURE OF THE DISEASE, AND OF LIFE OR DEATH, BY THE GOOD OR EVIL POSSESSION OF THE MOON AT THE TIME OF THE PATIENT'S FIRST LYING DOWN OR DEMANDING THE QUESTION.

Whosoever shall take his sick bed, the MOON in ARIES, decreasing in light and motion, and afflicted by the Conjunction, Quartile, or Opposition of SATURN: The first original of the disease is from a cold cause, with heavinesse of the head, weaknesse or dullnesse of the eyes, distellation of the humours from the head into the breast, throat and wind pipe stopped with flegm, the pulse weak and inordinate, more afflicted by night then by day; the inward parts very hot, but outward parts shivering with cold; a loathing in the stomach, with swoonings, and inordinate sweatings: If the MOON apply to none of the Fortunes, without doubt the sick will die; but if the MOON apply to the Fortunes, the sick shall recover, or at least he shall return from one disease to anotlier.

The MOON in ARIES afflicted of MARS, by Conjunction, Quartile or Opposition.

MARS afflicting, the MOON in ARIES, the disease is originally from some distemper in the membranes or pellicles of the brain, with continual Feavers, the sick taking no rest; their mouth and tongue exetream hot, dry and thirsty, a hot Liver, or inflammation thereof, with a drynesse in the breast; high pulses, keeping no order; a phrensie, of alienation of mind may justly be feared; Blood-letting and such things as refrigerate and mitigate, are convenient; if LUNA next after her separation from MARS, apply to an ill aspect of SATURN, viz. Conjunction, Quartile, or Opposition, there is small hopes of life; but if she be with, or apply to a good aspect of the fortunes, the sick shall recover.

The MOON in TAURUS, afflicted of SATURN, by Conjunction, Quartile, or Opposition.

The disease proceedeth from much luxury, surfeits, or too much repletion, causing Feavers, proceeding from

113

obstructions and distempers of the precordiacks, and arteries, with inflammation of the whole body, and uxulceration of the lungs; the pulse is high and inordinate; blood-letting and such medicines as purge or dissolve grosse humours are good; if the MOON be not helped by some good aspect of the fortunes, the sick will hardly escape, but if as aforesaid, in good aspects, judge the contrary.

The MOON in TAURUS, afflicted by MARS, by Conjunction, Quartile, or Opposition.

The disease proceedeth of too much ill blood, with continual Feavers, the whole body obstructed, inflammation of the neck, throat, and hinder part of the head, ache of the bones, inordinate watching, a desire to drink water, and cool things; blood-letting, and things that do cool, extenuate and mitigate, are convenient; if that the violence of MARS be not repelled by some of the fortunes, the sick will hardly live to the ninth day; but if the MOON be with either of the fortunes, expect recovery after the sixth day.

The MOON in GEMINI afflicted by SATURN, by Conjunction, Quartile or Opposition.

The Original of the sicknesse is from weariness of mind, by overburdening the same with multiplicity of care, or business, or by some wearinesse in travel, or over-watching; a small Feaver, the pain all over the body, but most in the joynts and arteries: after the third day the disease will increase to the 30. Inclines a consumption, with pulse rare and small, frequent sweating and pain of the Spleen, worse in the night then in the day. If MARS also afflict the MOON, the sick will not live above ten dayes, except a good aspect of JUPITER or VENUS intervene, and then after a long time the sick party may recover.

The MOON in GENINI, afflicted of MARS, by

Conjunction, Quartile or Opposition.

A most violent and dangerous Feaver, much obstruction, very high and disorderly pulses, Blood-letting is good for such; if LUNA have no assistance from the Fortunes, and apply to an ill-aspect of SATURN, the sick will hardly escape; but if LUNA shall be irradiated by the Fortunes, they shall recover.

The MOON in CANCER afflicted by SATURN, by Conjunction, Quartile, or Opposition.

Whosoever is taken sick, LUNA being in CANCER infortunated by SATURN, usually the disease is caused by a vehement cold, taken, much afflicted with melancholy matter, or with flegm, and distillations unto the breast, abundance of moysture, Catarrhs, Hoarseness, the passages are obstructed, Feaverish; and if the MOON have no help from the Fortunes, nature shall be overcome of the disease.

The MOON in CANCER, afflicted of MARS, by Conjunction, Quartile, or Opposition.

The sick hath taken some surfeit, much sweet flegm in the stomack, much blood, with eversion or turning of the ventricile; To vomit is good, as also things that refrigerate and cool; if the
MOON be decreasing in light and motion, and have no help from JUPITER or VENUS, the sick will hardly escape.

The MOON in LEO, in Conjunction, Quartiles or Opposition of SATURN.

When at the Decumbiture the MOON is in LEO, afflicted of SATURNE, the cause of the sicknesse is abundance of bad blood; the Patient will be oppressed with heat about the brest, with violent Feavers, troubled pulses, great heat, both inward and outward; Things that gently moisten, and heat, and mitigate, are good; when the MOON comes to the Opposition of SATURN, if JUPITER and VENUS assist not, usually the sick party is overcome of the disease.

The MOON in LEO, in Conjunction, Quartile, or Opposition of MARS.

When the MOON is afflicted of MARS in LEO, expect abundance of blood, causing strong Feavers, very weariness, and a strong delerium, no appetite, heavinesse over all the whole body, with drowsinesse and deep sleep, danger of a Consumption, and many and great distempers of the heart. Things that are refrigerative and restringent, are medicinable; the Conjunction and Opposition of MARS to the MOON, is more to be feared in this sign then in any other of the Zodiack; usually without the amicable aspects of the fortunes, the sick dieth about the ninth day.

The MOON in VIRGO, of SATURN, oppressed by Conjunction, Quartile, or Opposition.

The cause of. the distemper is taw crudities, and evil digestion of the stomack; much viscous flegm, head-ache, and pains under the ribs, inordinate Feavers; Things that do califie, mollifie, and dissolve, are convenient; if the MOON be not adjuvated by the Fortunes, the sick will be in danger about the 14th day; but if she be in conjunction with JUPITER and VENUS, after a long time you may expect recovery.

The MOON in VIRGO of MARS oppressed by Conjunction, Quartile, or Opposition.

The disease is from fretting and exulceration of the Intestines, with a flux of the belly, small Feavers, the stomack loathing and abhorring meats, pulse little, eversion

of the ventricle: things that obstruct, and repel sharp
humours, are good; you may expect death within thirty
days if the fortunes help not.

The MOON in LIBRA, oppressed of SATURN, by Conjunction, Quartile, or Opposition.

Gluttony, Surfeits of Wine, or meats not fully
digested, is the cause of the Disease; (sometimes too much
venery); the breast is pained, and also the head; no appetite
to eat, a loathing in the stomack, nightly feavers, cough,
hoarseness, distillation of Rheums, pulses remiss. Things
that califie and heat, are proper; if the MOON at the same
time be combust, and have no help from the fortunes, death
may be feared, more especially if MARS so also afflict the
MOON.

The MOON in LIBRA, oppressed of MARS, by Conjunction, Quartile, or Opposition.

Much blood offends the sick, causing intense
Feavers, with high pulses, much waking, and the whole
body in flames; things causing sleep, and blood-letting are
good; without the help of one of the fortunes, the sick will
be in great danger when the MOON comes to the body of
MARS.

The MOON in SCORPIO, afflicted by SATURN 's Conjunction, Quartile, or Opposition.

The disease is exulceration, or bubo's, near
the secrets, or in ANO OUT PUDENDO: If the MOON
increase in light and motion in aspect with JUPITER or
VENUS, the sick shall recover.

The MOON in SCORPION afflicted by MARS his Conjunction, Quartile, or Opposition.

117

When at the Decumbiture the MOON is afflicted
of MARS in SCORPIO, the disease doth proceed from
ulceration, or impostumation, the Pox, Hemorroids,
Pestilence, or the like, Measles in children,
Gonorrheas, &c. do afflict the sick party.

The MOON in SAGITTARIUS afflicted by SATURN'S Conjunction, Quartile, or Opposition.

The sick is much oppressed with a defluxion of thin, sharp,
and subtle humours, pain in the joynts and arteries, fear of a
Feaver, extremities of heat and cold, and sometimes the sick
hath Feavers with double accesse. Things that mitigate, heat
and moisten, and asswage, are good if they be given when
the MOON is in aspect with the fortunes.

The MOON in SAGITTARIUS, of MARS afflicted.

The oppression of the MOON in SAGITTARIUS by MARS,
declareth the Patient to be vexed with a most desperate
sickness; originally from gluttony, surfeiting, or overmuch
repletion, hath high Feavers, coming of choler, a flux of the
belly, the pulse weak. Things that cool and obstruct are
good; If the MOON be not beheld by the favourable aspects
of JUPITER or VENUS, the sick will hardly escape the 7th
day; but having past that day, there is great hope of
recovery.

The MOON in CAPRICORN, of SATURN afflicted by Conjunction, Quartile, or Opposition.

The disease is from a cold cause, with subtle and thin
distillations, heaviness of the breast, and the lungs
oppressed with difficulty in breathing, much troubles with
the Cough in the night-time, with intended Feavers.
Medicines that moderately heat and moisten, are

commendable; If the MOON be not helped by the fortunes, the sicknesse will be long, but not mortal.

The MOON in CAPRICORN, of MARS afflicted by Conjunction, Quartile, or Opposition

The sick is prone to vomit, caused by cholerick and bilious matter, or evil.digestion: the disease is very dangerous, an inappetency in the stomack, a swelling of the sinews, a flux of the belly follows, a cholerick humour offends the joynts, or fingers with ulceration; the pulses are remisse and slow; medicines that are obstructive and astringent, are convenient: If the MOON do not apply to the fortunes, the sick shall die when the MOON comes to MARS his Opposition; but if the violence of MARS be repressed by JUPITER or VENUS, after 7 days health shall be restored to the sick.

The MOON in AQUARIUS of SATURN, afflicted by Conjunction, Quartile, or Opposition.

The occasion of the sickness is from much labour, weariness, or watching, or for want of due refreshment of nature; the grief taketh the party unequal with remission and intension, until the MOON have passed her place in the Decumbiture; then being adjuvated by the Fortunes, health will be restored.

The MOON, in AQUARIUS of MARS, afflicted by Conjunction, Quartile, or Opposition.

If the MOON be decreasing in light and motion, and unfortunated of MARS, at any ones decumbiture, the infirmity proceeds from a most sharp and violent cause; taking the Patient with most vehement passions; any good Planet casting a favourable aspect to the MOON, at her

Quartile or Opposition to her place in the Decumbiture, the sick presently recovers after 20 days.

The MOON in PISCES of SATURN, afflicted by Conjunction, Quartile, or Opposition.

The distemper is caused from cold distillations, the party is molested with continual Feavers, often sighings under the breasts, extension of the precordiacks, and heart-strings. Things that do heat and mitigate, are convenient; if the MOON be not helped of the fortunes the sick will die when the MOON cometh to the Opposition of her place in the Decumbiture; but if she be in good aspect of JUPITER or VENUS, the sick shall recover after a long time, but the sickness leaveth pain and ache in the joynts and nerves.

The MOON in PISCES of MARS, oppressed by Conjunction, Quartile, or Opposition.

The body of the sick is full of grosse humours, caused by too much gluttony, and drinking or much repletion; the disease is most molested in the night, phrenzie or a delerium follows, sharp feavers, vehement thirst, and a desire of drink: Blood-letting is good in the beginning of the disease. If the MOON be not helped by good aspect of the fortunes, in the next Sextile to MARS, expect death; but if she have any aspect to JUPITER or VENUS, recovery is at hand.

Chapter XVI
Containing certain Observations taken out of CARDAN, and other expert Physitians.

The first observation is from AUGERIUS PERERIUS.

A Double Tertian invaded one ANNO 1547, April 23, at six in the morning, at which time MOON was in Conjunction with MARS; the 26th day having taken a purge the fever left him, the Quartile of the SUN and MOON that day was not much considerable, because they had no Aspect at the Decumbiture.

The 27, 28 and 29th dayes he seemed perfectly cured, nothing of the fever appeared perfectly remaining. The 30th day the Quartile of MARS excited a continued fever, with dangerous accidents; for on that day he began to rave and pull the bed-clothes, &c. but because the MOON in the

beginning of the Disease departed from the Conjunction of MARS to an Aspect of VENUS, all the symptomes became remiss and free from danger the 6th day of May, which was the 14th day from the decumbiture, at which time LUNA was in Trine to VENUS; neither could the Opposition of LUNA and MARS, the 8th of May prejudice, because LUNA separating from MARS applied to JUPITER and VENUS, for it's certain that the fortunes do help with what aspect soever they behold the Malevolents, or the MOON.

A Rational figure of the Decumbiture.

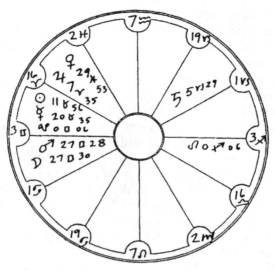

The second observation from CARDAN.

John Antoni of Campion (saith Cardan) being about 30 years
of age fell sick, occasioned by a journey: Until the fourth
day he seethed little oppressed, because LUNA was in
sextile with VENUS, and they in reception; MERCURY is
also in his own dignities, and LUNA being slow in motion,
the disease increased but slowly, for she was three days and
18 hours ere she came to 25" of GEMINI, wherein she was in
sextile to JUPITER and MARS (who are in conjunction) and
with fixed stars of moist natures, which caused great ardour
and turbulency in the urine, which began to appear the 5th
day. The 7th day the MOON by reason of her slow motion,
being now come to the Quartile of her place in the
Decumbiture, but onely to the beginning of LEO, he became
very ill, because she met with no good aspect, but was with
the Antiscion of SOL in the sixth, and the MOON's north
node in the

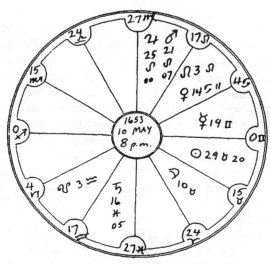

8th. The disease increased the 8th and 9th dayes, because LUNA was in Conjunction with JUPITER and MARS, among moist stars; he did sweat; for heat with moisture causeth sweat, and much Urine, which he also made. The 11th day he did sweat but with much diffculty, for LUNA was not yet free from the opposition of SATURN, to which succeeded a Sextile of VENUS. The 12th day he was exceeding ill and raved very much, but yet there did seem signs of Concoction in the –Urine. The 13th day he was no worse, notwithstanding VENUS' Sextile (who was inimical to the ascendant) because there was tendency to health. The 14th day he sweat again and somewhat better, the MOON having occurse to the Sextile of JUPITER, and of MARS, and to the Quartile of VENUS, and these caused heat. But the sicknesse could not then terminate, because the MOON had passed but 174 and 22 from her place at the beginning; therefore it was continued to the 17th day, whereon he was freed therefrom, the MOON having past her opposite place, and applyed to a Trine of VENUS.

The third Observation is also from CARDAN.

Liber II Chapter 16

The Decumbiture of one who dies the 14th day.
The MOON was in Quartile to VENUS at the beginning of
the disease, whose original was from a surfeit of meat and
drink, &c. he was immediately much oppressed by reason
the MOON was swift in motion. The 7th day he was
exceeding ill, the MOON was with her South Node and
void of any aspect of JUPITER, and applied to an
Opposition of VENUS, SOL being also in Quartile to
SATURNE. The 8th day he was somewhat better, having a
flux of blood at the nose: But yet strength failed, by reason
of the Opposition of VENUS' The 9th day he had some
respite, by reason of the Trine of the SUN. The 10th day the
MOON came to the Opposition of JUPITER and MARS. The
11th day he was near death, when the MOON came to the
Conjunction of SATURN at the tenth hour, and to the
Quartile of SOL the 18th hour. He died June 5th at nine
before noon, LUNA then coming exactly to her Opposition
place in the Decumbiture.

The cause of the disease may be seen in Chap. 9 of
HERMES TRISMECISTUS. And the Decumbiture was
mortal, as may appear by the 84th and 87th Aphorisms. The
Moon being not far from the cusp of the Ascendant, collects
the light of SATURN by Antiscion, and transfers the same to
VENUS in the 10th in Quartile to the Ascendant and Lady
of the 8th and although JUPITER behold LUNA and
Horoscope with a Sextile aspect, yet could he not help, but
only prolong the disease, because he was afflicted by MARS
his conjunction.

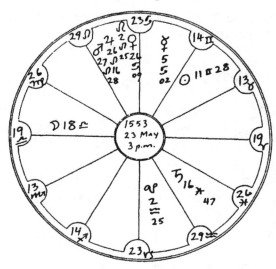

The fourth observation is from the same CARDAN.

BAPTIST CARDAN (a kinsman of CARDAN's) was run through the arm December 19, 1552 at 4h32 afternoon; when he received his wound whereof he died, he was 60 years of ago. When he was wounded MARS was near the North Node and LUNA near the South Node, and applying to the opposition of JUPITER unfortunate, and to the conjunction of SATURN; yet he was not immediately much oppressed, because the MOON is applying to a sextile of MERCURY, the wound being in the arme. The 4th day he was ill by reason of Quartile SOL, but yet without a fever, because no malevolenet did oppose; From hence to the tenth day he was so well that he arose from his Bed. The llth day at the third hour of the night he was greatly oppressed, when the MOON drew nigh to an opposition with the SUN, who was Anareta (because Lord of the opposite place of the MOON) the MOON and MERCURY were also in opposition. The 14th day from the time of the wound, he was taken with a fever, which was January 2nd. The 3rd of January when the MOON came to the body of

MARS he dyed. Thus CARDAN. Here are verified the 70th and 71st Aphorisms, and others.

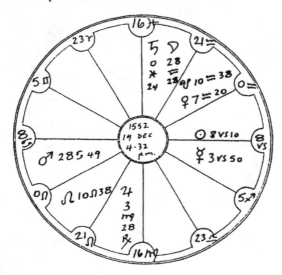

The fifth observation is from BODERIUS.

In the year 1545 (saith BODERIUS) I being much worried with a Diurnal fever, together with heaviness of my Breast and hypochondriacks, took my Bed on the day and hour hereafter mentioned, the MOON having separated from VENUS and MERCURY, and in the midst between the bodies of MARS and SOL, and in trine to JUPITER. Although the critical days were fortified with convenient aspects, yet they did not reduce my health; The significators in Tropical signes, the disease very often doth exceed a month. I was troubled with these distempers seven Weeks, and then they turned to a quatrain feaver, which held me about two years, the conjunction of SOL and VENUS did portend such a sickness, for MARS causeth acute diseases, and SOL chronicle, the MOON being in conjunction with

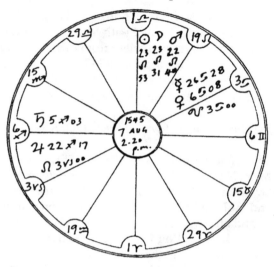

them did adde very much trouble to the length of the
disease; Many at that time were very much troubled with
the like disease, of whom that were in Years fell into
dropsies. All this being duely considered I had the advice of
many Physitians, who unanimously affirmed I would be
hydropical: Nature began to be somewhat raised, yet for
prevention I prepared a concoction of LIGNUS SANCTUS,
contrary to the advice of the Physitians, of which I drank
ten days to be bettered by it, and within a few months after
my body, which was nigh spent with these diseases, grew
healthy and perfectly amended.

      Thus one thing was unknown to me that
conjunction of SUN and MARS should portend quartain
fevers, chiefly MOON being in conjunction or aspect with
them. Thus BODERIUS.

      This is indeed a remarkable Decumbiture; and
many have admired it did not end in death suddenly, for
MARS & SUN with MOON quickly terminate the disease
with destruction; but being JUPITER Lord of the Horoscope

was safe and powerful in his own house, and angular, beholding the Luminaries joyned with MARS in a Trine, he would doubtless preserve the patient from death, but not without a long sickness: it was so that SATURN, who was the cause of the quartain was mitigated by VENUS. SATURN in the ascendant causeth long sicknesses always.

The 6th observation from the same BODERIUS.

A certain Priest fell sick of a diurnal Fever, 1551, August 30th, the MOON in 17° VIRGO, being not one degree separated from the SUN: about a month this disease much troubled and molested him: Then his diurnal fever turned to a tertian, and afterwards into aquartain; at last having brought up much by spitting 12 days before, the quartane left him. In brief, we may gather thus much, that the MOON being within the SUN's rayes combust, did indicate a malignant, but not mortal sickness.

Certainly we must acknowledge this Decumbiture to be a very dangerous one, for besides that LUNA was combust of SOL, within one degree of longitude (which in judgment might alone seem sufficient to destroy, as appears by the 85th Aphorism) both Luminaries were partly afflicted by the Opposition of SATURNE Lord of the Ascendant, and the SUN and MOON in the 8th house, agreeable to the 70th Aphorism. But JUPITER being very strong, and aspecting the Luminairies with a sextile, and Venus also afforded her assistance to the Horoscope by a Sextile, it was the less to be admired that after a long sickness the patient did recover. The MOON was separating from the SUN, and had North latitude, which made her be more occidental by three degrees,a which is very worthy consideration.

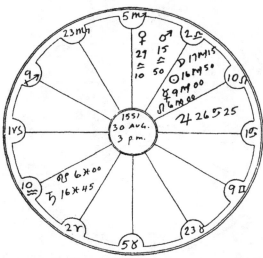

The seventh Observation is the Decumbiture of JOHN ANTONIO MAGINUS, the eminent MATHEMTATICIAN.

I began to be sick (saith he) of a quartaine fever, under this position of heaven, in which SATURN, author of the disease, and Lord of the ascendant was in the sixth, and the MOON separating from a Quartile of MARS, and sextile of the SUN, applied to a sextile of JUPITER her dispositor. By this sign might a long sickness be discerned, but to terminate in health at last: and that especially because JUPITER-- as radically posited, aspected SATURN with a Trine and the SUN in my Genesis, who is prorogator of life, is directed to the Trine of SATURN, in 11° LEO 20', and afterwards to the antiscion of VENUS, and Trine of MERCURY. In the figure of the Decumbiture SOL is in opposition to SATURN in the Radix, SATURN not being farre from the SUN, as may be seen in my Genesis, in our Tables of direction, being 1555, June 14th, 6h 57m pm. I was freed from this quartaine when the SUN came to the 29th degree of SAGITTARIUS, being the opposite place of SATURN at the beginning of the disease, and not far from

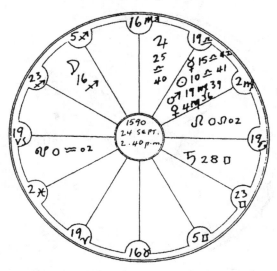

the sextile of JUPITER, at the Decumbiture; and that on the
11th of December the same year, for then I had my last fit,
neither was I ever after sensible of it; for on the 14th day of
the same moneth, when I expected my fit, there appeared
nothing of it. The SUN was then in opposition
SAGITTARIUS, separating from a Quartile of VENUS, and
applying to a sextile of the SUN, near her place in the
Decumbiture.

*The eighth Observation is of the Decumbiture of JOHN
BAPTISTA TRIANDULE, one of Verona.*

This is a very remarkable observation, for whilest
this unfortunate young man (being 28 years of age) was a
student at Padua, he received a dangerous wound in his
right knee, by means of which wound at length his whole
leg was amputated; and though he was most grievously
afflicted, so that Physitians did often despair of his life; yet

130

notwithstanding he recovered and lived about two years, going upon a wooden leg.

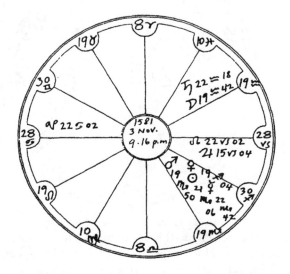

Whether therefore you take the SUN or MOON to be dominators of the ascendant, it matters not much, for they are both afflicted by malevolents, the MOON by conjunction of SATURN, and the SUN by Conjunction of MARS; also the MOON by fire Quartiles of MARS, and the SUN by the quartile of SATURN, so that it is not to be admired that this young man was so much oppressed under so unfortunate a position of Heaven, which did not yet destroy him, because both the fortunes conspired to help the Luminaries to their mutual antiscions, VENUS afflicting the MOON, and JUPITER the SUN, did somewhat repress the force of the malevolents; of the progresse of the cure, and the time of recovery, I am ignorant, for I was more solicitous to see how the native's geniture did predict such an accident. The native was born 1554, DIE MARTIS, June 12th, 34 minutes after Sun setting.

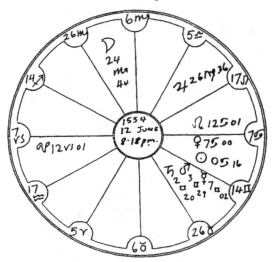

In this geniture there is no diversion of any signifier in the
Ecliptique agreeable to this accident, viz. the wound; for we
cannot take the Horoscope to the Trine of MARS, because
that will make the Geniture preceed the estimative time half
an hour, which is not probable.
Wherefore directing the Horoscope to the Quartile of MARS
in the Equator (according to our usual manner) it
anticipates the time estimative but 10 minutes and the event
doth very well answer hereunto, the Quartile of MARS
falleth in 331.28 and meeteth with the Horoscope in the
Ecliptique, with 10° and 26° AQUARIUS, the ark of diversion
being 27.25 which is equivalent to 27 years 5 months,
according to the common opinion.

      That MARS was author of the event, will appear
clearly, if we consider seriously his nature in this place,
being encompassed with any fixed stars of violent nature, as
the Hyades and stars of Orion with which he descendeth;
he is also in sextile with SATURN, he lived two years after
the wound, and then died a natural death (being aged 29
years) when LUNA the primary giver of life was directed to
the Quartile of SATURN in the Equator, which happened in

269.53 thereof, the MOON's circle or position is almost 24 and her oblique ascension 240.22 which subtracted from the fore mentioned Quartile, leaveth the ark of direction 29.31. The SUN also applied to a sextile of MARS at the time of death.

Presages of life and death, by the body of the Patient being sick.
Two ways did the famous HIPPOCRATES leave posterity, for the judging of the life and death of sick people; one by the Celestial aspects of the Planets, and the other by the Symptomes of the body of the man lying sick. The latter of these must first be performed; the profit of which, for 'tis good for something, according to HIPPOCRATES, is first the credit of the Piss: for first of all, hence avoids defamation, evil speeches and reproaches; the world shall never say he is a Dunce.

2. It will better his own knowledge, he need not apply living medicines to a dying man. Secondly, for the profit of the sick , hereby you may give them warning of death before it comes, and they will the more confidently commit themselves to the hands of a Physitian, when they know he knows something.

If the credit of HIPPOCRATES may passe for starling, he protests that what I here write, was confirmed in all his practices in Ethiopia, Libya, Mauritania, the Isle of Delos, Schythia, and Italy.

And he that diligently observes these, and compares them with the aspects of heavenly bodies, can never without a miracle fail in his judgment upon diseases. For my own part, dare commend the greatest part of them for authentick, though I have not made trial of them all; yet 'tis very probable, set the antiquity of the Author aside, that the meanest of them (if well heeded) may make a more infallible judgement upon a disease, then a whole tub full of Physitians.

I have somewhat inverted HIPPOCRATES order; and my reason was, because I would bring the businesse into one single ingresse, and make them as plain to the meanest capacity as a pike-staff; and if they cannot understand them, as I have committed them to posterity, the fault is in the dulnesse of their own wits, and there let it rest.

HIPPOCRATES divides them into three books, and in that I will follow him to a hair.

The first book I will divide into these parts: presages of disease.

1- The face
2- The eyes and lips
3- The manner of lying
4- The teeth
5- Ulcers, or Issues
6- The hands
7- The breath
8- The sweat
9- Tumours and Aposthumes.

Chapter 1.
Presages by the Face

1. If in a sick body the face look as it did of health, or but little different, the hope of recovery is not small: signs of death in the face of a sick body are these:

1. The nostrils are extenuated and very sharp.

2. The eyes are hollow.

3. The skin of the Fore-head or eye-brows, hard, dry, and loose; and looks as though it were tan'd.

4. The ears are cold, shrunk, and almost doubled.

5. The face is black, pale, or swarthy, or deformed; He looks but ilfavouredly.

If these, or most of these appear (be not too rash neither, for rashness is the daughter of ignorance; but be sober minded) and first enquire whether the patient hath not fasted much, or wanted sleep, or had a flux a long time:

If these, or any of these had not a being before the sickness, the danger of death is to be feared.

If the sickness have been four or five dayes, before you see these Symptoms, they are but the harbingers of death, and he follows them at the tail.

Chapter 11.
Presages by the eyes and lips.

1. Signs of death by the eyes are: if they be deprived of sight, or weep against the patient's will.

2. If they seem as though they would fall out of his head.

3. When one of the eyes becomes less then the other.

4. When the white of the eyes become reddish.

5. When they are blear-ey'd, or dim-ey'd, and not used to be before.

6. When they are very moveable, gashful, staring up and down, or sunk deep into the head.

7.When the sick grows squint-ey'd, and not so before, and stares up and down as though he was frighted.

8. When the patient sleeps with his eyes open, and was not so accustomed to do.

Then enquire if these come not by flux, nor laxative medicines; If not, they are signs of death.

9. When the eye-lids, nose and lips, are crooked, or drawn in to one side.

10. If the lips are thin, cold, pale, and hanging down, and the nose very sharp, it denotes death.

Chapter 111.
Presages by the manner of lying in Bed.

It is best when men lye in bed in that form in sickness as they did when they were in health, mortal signs are first.

1. When the neck, hands, and feet are extended stiff and inflexible, not to be moved.

2. Sudden starting up out of the bed.

3. Casting their head down to the feet of the bed.

4. Sleeping with their mouth open, contrary to former custome.

5. To using and tumbling, or throwing himself from one end of the bed to the other, shews the man in terrible condition, if not in a dying condition.

6. To sleep with the belly downward, contrary to custome, skews aches of the belly, or little less then madness.

7. If the desire in sickness be to go out of one room into another, mistake the room for a world.

8. He that is impatient and forceth himself to rise upon a Critical day, puts himself in great danger; if the disease be violent and touch his Lungs, the Critical day may prove mortal.

Chapter IV.
Presages by the teeth.

1. Gnashing of teeth in a Fever, if not naturally, is a dangerous sign.

2. If withal he be deprived of his senses, and his sickness only a fever, not a Frenzy, and gnashing his teeth; he calls for death, and he will quickly come.

Chapter V.
Presages by Ulcers and Issues.

If a sick person have an Ulcer or Issue, whether it came before the sickness, or with it; (there is not a halfpenny to chuse) and it dry up and become green, black, or swarthy, if the patient become worse and worse, Doctor death is coming to cure him.

Chapter VI.
Presages by the Hands.

1. If in fevers, or any other acute diseases, frenzy excepted, the sick by pedling or plucking the bed-cloths, or pulling straws, if he could find them, a thousand to one he live the age of a little f ish. Judge the life, if he take violent hold of the bed-cloths, ceiling, or wall.

Chapter VII.
Presages of the Breath.

By the breath is best judgement given upon the spirits, heart, and lungs.

If the disease have invaded the spirits, (and that is the quickest way to kill a man) carry aUrinal full of Pisse to the Doctor, and he will say, He ails nothing; the reason is, there is no digestion found in the Urine; because the disease seizeth not the body, but the spirits. A man is troubled in mind, his Wife and Children do not please him; being troubled, is sick for madness; his Wife, as bad as she is, loves him, and will carry his Pisse to the Doctor; he looks upon it and will drink the man as well as himself (and that is bad enough) only his trouble is so great, he knows as much by his Urine, as if he had looked into a Crows nest; he bath no more skill in Astrology, then I have in making Candles; the man speaks out all the wit at once, and saith, her husband ails nothing, it may be he ails nothing, but only to be out of the world; the drift of this
discourse,_is only to shew you some diseases seize only upon the spirits, others only upon the body. To this purpose.

1. The distance between breathing; if it be too long, and coldness of the breath, shews death is not above two or three foot off; gentle breath in hot diseases is an argument of death.

Chapter VIII.
Presages by Sweat.

Those kind sweats which happen upon Judicial or Critical days, are wholsome, commendable, and good, for they are sent by Doctor Health.

If sweat by universal 'tis excellent; and if the Patient mend by his sweating, 'tis a for-runner of a Cure.

3. Mortal sweats are first of all cold.

4. Only in one part of the body, usually the forehead and face; if the Patient afflicted by such sweats die not, his disease will continue longer then he would have it.

Chapter IX.
Presage by Tumours.

1. If the Patient that lieth sick of a Feaver, feeleth neither pain, inflammation, tumour, nor hardnesse upon or neer about his ribs, 'tis a very good sign.

2. If any of these be there, and upon both sides, 'tis but a bad sign at the best.

3. If he feels great motions and pulsations in one of his sides it prognosticates great pain and depravation of his senses.

4. If with this pulsation, his eyes move faster then they should do, the Patient is in danger to fall into a frenzy, if not to mischief himself.

The last Chapter of Aposthumes.

1. The Collection of an Aposthume in both sides in a burning Feaver, is more dangerous then it had been but upon one side; for two men will sooner kill a man then one.

2. 'Tis more dangerous on the left side then on the right.

3. If it continue 20 days, and the Feaver ceaseth not, neither the Aposthumes diminisheth, it will come to maturation.

4. If there come a Flux of blood through the nose upon the first critical day, it easeth the Patient; only he will be pained in his head, and troubled with dimnesse of sight at noon day, chiefly if he be about thirty, or thirty-five years of age.

5. When the Aposthume is soft, and with pain when 'tis handled, it requires a longer time to cure then the former did, but not half so dangerous.

6. Such a one may continue two moneths before it comes to be ripe.

7. The Aposthume that is hard, great, and painful, if it be not mortel, I am sure it is dangerous.

8. Aposthumes of the belly are never so great as they that grow under the midrife; and yet those that grow under the Navel are lesse then they, and usually come to Suppuration.

9. 'Tis a good sign when they purge by a Flux of blood in the nostrils.

10. Some Aposthumes purge only outwards, and they are little, round, and sharp pointed; and they are most healthful, lesse mortal.

11. Such as are large, grosse, or round, but flat, are most dangerous.

12. Those that purge, and break within the belly and make tumours outwardly, are as bad as the Devil himself, or ROBIN GOODFELLOW, and are very pernicious; those that make no tumour outwardly, excel them as far as the shot of a Cannon doth that of a Pistol.

13. The matter which comes out of the Imposthumes , being white, and not unsavoury, is very good and he a healthful.

14. The more the colour differs from white, the worse it is; and thus much for the first book.

The Second Hook of the Presages of HIPPOCRATES, you
shall find marshalled in this order

Chapter l.
Presages by Dropsies in Fevers.

First, all manner of Dropsies in Fevers are dangerous, if not
mortal, I know you would fain know a reason: I'le tell you; a
Fever proceeds of heat, Dropsies of cold: And as fire and
water agree, so doth fever and Dropsie; and what you give
to mitigate a feaver, encreaseth a Dropsie; a Dropsie and
Fever agree like fire and water; the SUN having drawn up a
fiery quality from the earth, and envelloped it round with a
cloud of snow, thence comes lightning and thunder, and
terifies the people; and as well doth a Fever and Dropsie
agree in microcosms, as fire and water doth in the Region of
air; many men know there is a middle Region in the ayr, but
few know what it is, and as little where, onely a few sons,
whom mother wisdom bath instructed in it.
2. If the Dropsie and a Fever meet in one body
they will play reakes as sometimes they doe, though
not often) the Liver pays all the score.

3. If afflictsthe VENA LECTUA, and most commonly
the guts themselves; the legs are presently
tormented, and they cannot march handsomly; a flux
follows, and the swelling in the belly is not a whit lessened
by it.

4.If the Liver be most afflicted, the Patient hath got a dry
cough, and he knows not how to help it; he spits but very
little, and wishes he could spit more; the belly is very hard,
and it goes to stool, 'tis with more pain, then he would
willingly endure; his feet swell, there is tumours,
inflammation in his sides, sometimes they dissipate, and
sometimes they swell again.

Chapter 11.
Presages of Life and Death in Fevers.

1. When the Patient is cold on his head or face, or bath cold
sweats there: Also if his hands and feet be cold, but his belly
and sides hot and burning, the case is extream dangerous,
and is a sign that death bath taken possession of the house
and clay where life formerly had dwelt.

2. It is a helpful sign in a fever, when all the parts of the
body are equally hot, though they be something hotter then
they should be.

3. The body heavy, the nailes of a leaden swarthy colour,
the disease will be cured by death, and not by physick.

4.Induring of a sickness without anguish, shews strength of
nature; and so long as she holds up her head, there is some
hopes.

5. Let .every one that views a Patient, if he would act the
part of a wise man, enquire after the custome of the man's
body when he was in health; and if his spittle, sleep, or
excrement, &c. be as they were when the body was in
health, recovery is coming, and it comes apace, and will
speedily be with the sick for his comfort.

The more these signs differ in sickness from what they were
in health, the more is the danger.

6. By these signs you may also know, in some

measure, what part of the body is afflicted, and
by what humour, if you cannot, go to the school
of dame Nature, she is an excellent School-mistress.

Chapter III.
Presages by the Testicles.

When the Yard and Testicles are shrunk in, and apparently
diminished against nature, it signifies great pain and
anguish and death followes them at the heeles as swift as
the wind.

Chapter IV.
Presages of Sleeping.

First of all, when the sick sleeps in the night and keeps
walking in the day, this is usually a lovely hopeful sign of
recovery to the sick, the reins of government are not yet
forced out of the hands of dame nature, and she, if she be
not hindered by intemperance, or other impediments,
governs prudently.

2. Although it be not altogether wholesome to sleep from
the break of day till eight or nine of the clock in the
morning; Yet it is more commendable to sleep then, then
any other time of the day.

3. Continual watching is extream dangerous, and cries aloud
that deprivation of senses is at hand, if it be not already
come.

Chapter V.
Presages by excrements of the belly in Fevers.

First of all, the most commendable sign is when he
that is surprized with a fever, retains the same custome in
avoyding his excrements which he ordinarily used when his
body was best health.

2. Alwayes in excrements you must regard the quality and
quantity of dyet; for take this for a certain rule, and you
shall find it never vary without a miracle, how much the
excrements are different from that, so much worse is the
sign.

3. Laudable excrements are neither too thick nor too thin, yet it is worse that they be too thick, then too thin; for astringency in a fever is naught and not to be allowed. He is fitter to make a Hangman then a Physitian that takes no care that his patient goe orderly to stool.

A looseness in a fever proclaims to the world that the patient kept ill diet before.

4. It is exceeding good that the colour of the excrement be according to the food taken.

5. It is very good that the Patient go to stool without pain, for if nature is troubled to expel natural excrements, she will find a harder pull of it to expel the disease.

6. If excrements be liquid, viz. if the man that is sick of fever have a looseness, and what comes from him, come without violence, pain or wind, it is a hopeful sign, for nature hath found out a way to turne out the disease at the back-door.

7. Yet I beseech you to take notice of this; frequent going to stool weakens the sick, spoils the digestion, mars the retentive faculty, makes the sick forward and faint.

8. Worms coming forth of the body with excrements at the end of the malady, is a good sign and hopeful; but at the beginning of the sickness 'tis desperate; the poor Worms know when nature is decaying, and therefore leave the body before it is breatliless.

Here's a strange thing, that the worms have as much knowledge as a physitian.

9. It's very good in every sickness, when the belly is soft, and not puffed up, with wind: Wind is an active creature, and playes reakes in the body of man when it gets where it should not be.

10. The excrements when they are very watery,

white, or very red and frothy, they are very dangerous.

By the leave of HIPPOCRATES, not always mortal.

11. Excrements black, green, or slimy, give you fair warning, if any warning will serve the turn, that the disease may end in death, and that's most probable.

12. Mixture of the forenamed colours is no lesse dangerous, but skews longer continuance of the disease: in the former the sick runs to his grave as hard as lie can drive; in this he walks to the same place, as though he told his steps.

13. When little skins like the peeling of guts come forth of the excrements, the disease is dangerous. This symptome was ordinarily seen in the Epidemical disease in London, 1649 which so puzzled the Colledge of Physitians, that their learned ignorance was so far from curing of it, that they could not tell what it was.

For Mr. CALLEN (for they know not where Dame Nature, the mother of Physitians dwells) instructed them in no such principles.

Mine own son, about three years of age, was taken of the same disease, my self being in the Country, when the hopes of life was but small I was sent for up: what came from him (and that was once in a hour) was wrapt round in skins.

I cured him by only boyling Mallows in his drink: and to manifest my thankfulness to God for so great a mercy, I here declare it to the world.

Chapter VI
Presages by wind in the Bowels and Womb.

First of all, wind issuing out gently and voluntarily, is the best and most wholesome sign.

2. Worse then that, when it comes forth with pain and griping.

3. Worst of all, when it is retained, and cannot come out at all, but causes swellings there.

4. Swellings of the wind in the belly according to
HIPPOCRATES, are best cured by expulsion downward,
or by Urine; thus my Author.

I care not greatly if I relate the cure done in such a
case, by one of the wisest Physitians that the SUN shone
upon in England, Dr. BUTLER of Cambridge. A gentleman
was possessed with wind in his belly; a great inflammation
there was there. The Doctor comes to him, and perceiving
the original of it was wind, for he was a man of penetrating
judgement, calling for a rolling-pin; The man was never
subject to covetousnesse, and as little to pride: Down turns
he the cloaths from the bed: up he gets boots and all, not
regarding the Holland-sheers; and falls to rolling the mans
belly with a rolling-pin; the Patients fundament sounds an
alarm, and certifies all the company that ease was a coming.

Chapter VII.
Presages by the Urine in a Feaver.

First of all, if the Urine in a Feaver, or any other sickness,
have residence near the bottome, in colour white, in form
like a Piramid.

2. So much the more the Urine differs from this, so much
the worse he is.

3. Grosse resolutions, like dust or bran in the bottoms of the
Urine, is a very evil sign.

But 'tis worse then that when they are like scales of fish.

4. The Urine white and clear signifies melancholy, and is
very bad; for if the retentive faculty be caused by
melancholy, the disease is like enough to hold long, for
melancholy will retain as well what it should not, as what is
should.

5. A cloud hanging in the Urine signifies health if it be
white; if it be black, 'tis dangerous; and then your mother
wit will tell you, that the blacker it is, it is the more
dangerous.

6. The Urine yellow, very clear and subtile, skews the
sicknesse will continue longer then the sick party would

willingly have it; crudity and digestion hath taken occasion
to shoulder out health.

7. In such a case there is fear, and that not a little, lest the
sick die before the humour come to concoction; what a
trick's that to cut off nature before she can do her business ?
and let me tell you this, I knew a man in LONDON, that
shall be namelesse, that was furious mercilesse pestilential
Feaver; his Urine was according to this Aphorism, he had a
swelling in his Emunctuary of, the brain, (viz.) under his
ear.

It arose as fairly as fair could be even till the hour of his
death, yet he died; nature did the best she could to expel the
disease, but she was anticipated: did you never know a man
die in the prime of health ? if not, go to St. Tyburn, and you
may be informed.

8. Slimy, muddy, black, tawny dirty, filthy, stinking Urine, is
usually mortal.

9. If a childs Urine be brought to you, and it look pale and
deer, like Conduit water, it is very bad; I know you long for
a reason, you shall not lose your longing; I told you before
such a humour was the badge of a melancholy
disposition; youth is naturally hot and moist; melancholy,
cold and dry, ERGO; extream inimical to youth.

10. If you spy in the Urine a thing like a cob-web swimming
on the top, it is bin a scurvy sign.

11. Thick Urine signifies but a thin body, for he that made it
hath a consumption.

12. White clues in the Urine, aud neer the bottome, are
commendable; black clouds, and neer the top, are bad and
vituperous.

In all these have regard to the bladder; for if that be
diseased, all these presages are in vain.

Thus HIPPOCRATES: the truth is, many of them
seem to me pretty rational, neither am I able to contradict
the rest, as I have been a Piss-Prophet all my life: yet this I
know to be true, and Doctor Experience is my witnesse, that
if the man he sick of a Feaver, and the Urine appears like

the Urine of a healthy man, as I have known it in more then one, and by this argument will I prove very uncertainty in Urine, death's a coming, provide for him.

I spake with Doctor Reason at the same time, for they two brethern seldom go asunder; and he told me the reason was because the disease workt upon the spirits, and not upon the body; and that's as ready a way to kill a man as to chop off his head.

Chapter VIII.
Presages of Vomiting in Feavers.

First, to vomit up flegm and choler in a Feaver, is a very good sign, because they are better out of your body then in it; they are but scurvy inmates when they keep not their proper place.

2. If what be vomited be green, livid, or black, 'tis dangerous.

3. If it be mixed or compounded of these, 'tis mortal.

4. If it stink, so that you cannot endure to hold your nose over it, and have but one of these colours, death comes gallowping: Thus HIPPOCRATES.

HIPPOCRATES was a brave Physitian, I confesses GALEN mended his works in Physick, just as ARISTOTLE mended PLATO's in Phylosophy, and that is as sour Ale mends in sunimer.

Chapter IX.
Presages by Spittle in Feavers.

1. Spittle in all diseases of the lungs, and maladies under the ribs, if it come in the beginning of a disease, without pain, of such a colour as spittle should be, well digested, not vicious, it's very commendable, there's some hopes of it.

2. If the spittle come not up without vehement coughing, it's an ill sign when nature is forced by violence to cast out her enemy.

3. White spittle, tough and knotty, is very dangerous in a Feaver; but when men spit blood it's worse, and yet such things happen sometimes.

4. If the spittle be green or fleshy, it gives notice of a bad and ill-conditioned sicknesse.

5. Black spittle is the worst of all, for then grim death's a coming.

6. When the matter which should be spit out, remains still within the lungs, and troubles the windpipe, there's but little security of life: and I am confident never a one of the Colledge keeps an insurance office for such a businesse, nor will ensure thereupon at 50 per cent.

7. What we told you was wholesome at the beginning of the malady, if it continue longer then the first Crisis, it's suspicious, if it be not dangerous.

8. If the pain be eased by spitting, it's very good, let the wind blow which way it will: and then

9. If the spittle be black, and if the spittle do foreshew death, it is that yet if the pain be eased by it, though I cannot say it is hopeful, yet this I say, it is lesse dangerous.

Chapter X
Presages by Sneezin & in Feavers.

1. Sneezing in hot maladies, let the malady be as dangerous as a halter, it is hopeful and commendable, and may procure a reprieve.

2. yet in maladies of the lungs, if it come with much rheum, and pain be felt after, it is dangerous, come it when it will, whether in the fit, or presently after.

Chapter XI.
Presages of Suppuration in Aposthumes.

1. If the pain of an Imposthume cease not by spitting, to which add laxative medicines, and letting blood, 'tis forty to one if it come not to suppuration.

2. When the Aposthume breaketh, the spittle giving notice of choler, whether matter come out with the spittle, or after, it is dangerous.

3. If the matter come upon the first Crisis, it comes to tell you death will come upon the second Crisis, unlesse the Physitian be all the wiser to stave him off: doth there not such a one live in the AMEN-CORNER ?

4. If the former Aphorism appear, and other healthful signs appear together with it, Dame nature may happen to help her self, and never be beholding to the Colledge; and if you'l be ruled by me, take acquaintance with her: and that you may do so, I'le describe her to you, that you may know her when you meet her in the street: She's a plain homely woman in a beggarly contemptible condition, regarded by none (unlesse it be the children of wisedom) she hath truth written upon her brest; those that think themselves wise tread her under boot; she carries Dr. Reason in her right hand, and Dr. Experience in her left; her head is round about with the eternal providence, and in her brain is written the knowledge of all things, in words at length, and not in figures; she always goes towards Heaven, and if you ask her, she'l bid you come after: God is her father, and her mother's name is the good of the creation; if you follow her, you shall not want; she treads upon the world, and looks upward; she is a virgin, a wife, and a widow; if she give you a paper in your hand,

in which is written KNOW THY SELF; she hath no money, yet is Mistress of the mines in India; in all her words you shall find more truth then eloquence; if you please to ask her for her Commission, she will shew it signed by JEHOVAH, not by ARISTOTLE or GALEN. Her ways are very plain, you may find them in the darkest night, without a candle and lanthorn; she is always everywhere, and yet still with me, she's my mother; she's a woman and yet an Academick; she's present to all that call upon her, yet not Ubiquitary; she always weeps, and yet I never saw her laugh. I hope none will blame me for writing this description of my Mother, so much despised, so little thought on by the Rabbies of our age. NOVERINT UNIVERSE PERI PRESENTES, that she is my Mother, and her two sons, Dr. Reason, and Dr. Experience, my brethren.

Chapter XII
Presages by the time of the Ruptures of Aposthumes.

1. That all Aposthumes have not one and the same time of maturation, is so certain, that it needs no further dispute of the story.

2. It is most usual and most wholsome for Aposthumes to break upon judicial days; what they be, and when they happen, you know already, unlesse you began at the latter end of the Book first. HIPPOCRATES reckons them by number of days, 'tis true; but so have not I, but by the course of the MOON. Do not blame HIPPOCRATES for a small fault; rather think your selves engaged to him for doing any thing; it may be 'twas GALEN's fault, not his.

3. Take notice that HIPPOCRATES was guided by good principles; for he tells you that the beginning of the disease is, when the Patient feels heat, a fever, stiffnesse, pain, pricking, or any thing else that denotes a disease-

4. When you feel that, do but so much for me as to make that time the basis to prognosticate the event.

5. Coughing, spitting, and spawling, pain difficulty of breathing, are true prognosticks that the Aposthume is neer breaking.

6. As by the Forlorn hope you may fudge what the Army is, so by these signs you may judge of the greatnesse of the Aposthume.

7. As by a Citizens spending you may judge how long he will hold; so by the swiftnesse of those signs you may judge how soon the Aposthume will break.

8. Sometimes the Aposthume breaks, and life is undone by it; sometimes it breaks, and death runs away for fear of the noise. 'Twere worth the while to know how this might be

known; I'le tell you how, and never go so far as
AMEN-CORNER for it either.

If when the Aposthume's broken, the man begins to
fall to his victuals, and feed like a Farmer; if the matter be
white, equal, salt, and come out without pain, take these to
be signs of speedy health, and say I told you so.
9. If the Fever cease not, or ceasing come with a fresh
supply, 'twere worth the while to know whether it will
return again or no; I'le tell you how to know, (if you will but
read it). If the Fever will return again, the thirst remains still
to keep possession: and when the Fever doth return again,
the faeces being very watry, green, livid or slimy, fortifie
against death, for he is not far off.
10. If the Patient feel pain in both sides, both sides are
Aposthumated; wherefore do they ache else think you ?
11. If he feels more pain in one side, then on the other, cause
him to lie on the soundest side: if he feel heaviness there, be
sure there is an Aposthume also.
12. If some good signs appear, and some bad, compare them
all together, and judge by most testimony; make use of all
the rules you can, that so you may find the truth, and avoid
infamy.

Chapter XIII
Presages of Aposthumes about the Ears.

First, when Aposthumes which come either about
or under the ears, come to maturation and break, the
bitternesse of death is past.
2. You may know when there's an Aposthume there, by
swelling and pain, by heat and burning, by rednesse of
colour, and inflammation about the place.

Chapter XIV
Aposthumes in the feet.
1. In vehement and dangerous diseases of the lungs, it
conduceth much to the help of the Patient when small
Pustules or Aposthumes appear in the feet.

2. If withal the spittle change from red to white, it gives certain testimony that recovery approacheth.

3. If the spittle turn not from red to white, then the pain ceaseth not, and the sinews of the part Aposthumated, are in danger of shrinking.

4. If together with the former, the Aposthumes also vanish away, the man loseth his senses first, and his life afterwards.

5. Aged people are more usually troubled with the diseases in the lungs, then young people.

6. It's very dangerous in all Aposthumes when the pain ascends Upwards.

7. Easie spitting white spittle, and not stinking, is a commendable sign in all diseases of the lungs; but if spittle be red, black, or stinking, 'tis deadly.

Chapter XV.
Presages by the Bladder in Fevers.

1. First, hardnesse and pain in the Bladder in quotidian Fevers, usually foreshews death is approaching.

2. If withal the Urine be stopped, judge the like.

3. In Aposthumes of the Bladder (when they come to scurvy places) if the Urine be like matter of the Aposthume, and the pain cease, and .the Fever mitigate, and the Bladder be molified; when you see these signs, you may be confident the worst is past.

4. This disease usually happens to few, but children, and to them most usually about the seventh and fourteenth years of their age.

The third book of the Presages of HIPPOCRATES.

    This Book I confess, is but short, yet the better order it is in, the handsomer will it look; and the reason is because God is the God of order.

    Let no man blame that gallant soul HIPPOCRATES for writing a little disorderly; rather let him bless God that he wrote at all: Let our Colledge of Physicians write so to purpose, and in their mother tongue, as he did in his; and

the rest of my days shall be spent in admiring and
applauding them.

But to return to my purpose, you shall find this third Book
presented to your view in this order-

1. Presages in Fevers 2. Quincies 3. The Uvula 4.Vomiting
in Fevers.

Of these in order.

Chapter 1
Presages in Fevers

1. This is most certain, and verified by continual experience,
that a Fever terminates in death to one, and in life to
another, in both upon one and the same day; and the
reason why, you may find in the beginnings of this book in
that part, the basest of which was borrowed from the
famous AVENERA.

2. Then will you see a reason, why it is as requisite to view
the body of the sick, as the position of the stars.

It is a custome in Italy, or at least it was but a few
years since, that a Physitian might not deny to view a sick
body, if he had but his fee given him, which amounted to 18
pence sterling. If he carried two Schollers with him, he had
12 pence more, if the Patient were willing to give it him:
which being added to the former, amounts just to 2 shillings
and six pence if he had carried twenty Schollers, he had no
more.

To the Patient comes he, for he dares not deny it,
whate're the disease be, if he be in health, and at liberty:
there doth he instruct the Schollers by the urine, by the
symptoms of the disease, its continuation and accidents, &c.
whether the sick be like to live or die; how the disease
opposeth nature, and which way.

This makes the Italian Physitians able men, when
the greatest part of ours are like to die dunces; who dares
deny, that has but wit to know his right hand from his left;
but that seeing the body, hearing the relation, and feeling
the pulse of the sick, is a better way to judge then gazing at
as much pisse as the Thames will hold ?

I wish from my heart our present State would take this matter into consideration, and take a little care for the lives of the poor Commonalty, that a poor man that wants money to buy his wife and children bread, may not perish for want of an Angel to see a proud insulting domineering Physician to give him a visit. I think it is a duty belonging to the Keepers of the Liberty of England. I would help my poor brethren in this particular if I could, but I cannot.

Whosoever reads what I have here written, and approves of it, let him joyn with me in a petition to the State, for the rectifying of this disorder.

Those who approve not of it, let them answer me to this Question, Who made a difference between the Rich and the Poor ? Was it God, or the World?

If the world, it is most certain then it will not stand; for the fashion of the world passeth away.

If many good signs appear at the beginning of a Feaver, note the sign and degree the MOON is in at the Decumbiture. And the party will recover when the MOON comes to the Sextile of the place she was in. HIPPOCRATES was an Astrologer, as appears by his Aphorism; And our Colledge, the Physitians, hug his writing under their arms, but follow him as much as the Pope follows Saint Peter.

4. Note the place the MOON is in at the Decumbiture, then view the sick body, when the MOON comes to the Sextile of that place: if you find ill Symptomes of the sick body, then you may fear death when she comes to the Quartile of that place, and you have cause enough.

5. Short Maladies are better judged of then long: a great deal of time may produce more alteration then a little.

6. If Fevers happen to women in child-bed, begin the Calculation at the time of her delivery, and not at the Initiation of the sicknesse, and take their Crisis that way.

7. If the Fever continue to the third Crisis, which is not often; you may presage bleeding at the Nose; and it is twenty to one it comes not upon the day of the third Crisis, or neer it.

8. If the Patient bleed at the Nose, be sure he hath an Imposthume in some of the inferiour part of the body.

9. Flux of blood in such a case most usually haps to people that are under thirty years of age; Imposthumes to them that are older.

10. If the sick find a vehement pain about his forehead, or place neer it, he is very subject to bleed at the Nose, and that may save his life.

11. Young persons oftner die at the first Crisis in Fevers then ancient; and the reason is, because their nature is hotter, and the more subject to take fire; for he that knows but his A.B.C. in Physick, knows a Fever comes of heat.

12. Old persons sooner die upon relapses then young; and the reason is, because their bodies are weaker.

13. Ulcerations in the throat are usually mortal in hot diseases.

14. Fevers continue longer in ancient people then they do in young; and the reason is, because the bodies of ancient people are colder; dry wood will burn most violently it is confest, but wet wood will be longer a burning.

15. Ancient people are more subject to Quartain Agues then young; and the reason is, because SATURN causeth them; a child will leave playing with his father, to play with his equals.

Chapter 11.
Presages of the Quinsey.

1. All Quinseys are extream dangerous, and sometimes Mortal.

2. The most dangerous signs in a Quinsey are great pain, great difficulty in breathing, yet no swelling outwardly appearing; or if the swelling appear, the external part. of the throat is most afflicted. And if you do not believe better to have the External part of the Throat afflicted then the Internal, I wish you did.

3. Here you find that in a Quinsey, it is usually better when they appear outwardly, then when they do not.

4. If the swelling appear not outwardly, they usually kill within four days at the furthest, although no Crisis come at that time. My own opinion is, though I hold an absolute truth in the Crisis, as I have laid them down in this book; yet withal I know as well that there is a difference to be made between the time that the disease overcome the vitals, and the time of the dissolution; as also, that in a proper acute disease. The MOON to the semi Sextile of the place she was in at the Decumbiture, often fills, because she is then a sign opposite in respect of nature, sex, and time.

5. If a red tumour appear outwardly, and fall in again, the danger of death is great: Life may borrow a little time, and so forth, but 'tis to be feered, though the Patient feel ease for the time.

Chapter III.
Presages by the Uvula.

The presages are few; happily honest HIPPOCRATES, whom Authors call divine, for his ingenuity rather then religion, did it because the diseases in this part of the body are but few, and those few appear but seldome.

1. Incision in the Uvula, Gargarion, or Columella, when it is swoln, red, or gross, is dangerous: Physitians love to trouble your pates with hard words; for if they would write plain English, they could not make silly people believe wonders, and then their DIANA would down; you shall find an explanation of all such words which he that can but read his Primer shall find at the latter end the book.

2. If the Uvula look pale or livid, and the upper part not swelled, you may make an incision without danger.

3. Be sure you purge the belly before you be too busie in making incision in those parts; Thus HIPPOCRATES. The truth is, I cannot find any reason why any incision at all should be made there: a man may as well plead Excise, as Custome for it, for ought I know.

If there be an inflammation there, blood-letting in the arm will serve the turn; if putrefaction, or ulcer, or sometimes happen to such, as our company of Chyrurgeons Flux for the French Pox, either for want of care or skill, or something else; cleansing medicines will do the deed. I do not in this Treatise professe to write an Anatomy; if I did, I could tell you what the use of the Uvula was, and how difficult an incision there is, and how dangerous the effects of it may prove; but I passe it and come to.

Chapter IV.
Presages of vomiting in a Fever.

First of all, when there appears black things, or things like flies before the eyes of him that hath a Fever, viz'. when he thinks he sees flies, when there's no such thing neer him, be sure the sick will vomit yellow choler, and the surer if withal he find an illnesse at his stomack.

2. If there be a stiffnesse and chilinesse in those parts near the Hypochondria, the vomiting will the sooner be hastened.

3. My Author doth not tell whether this vomiting be good or bad in a Fever: therefore I'le tell it you for him; It shews strength of nature, therefore take it as a hopeful sign; the choler which is vomited up lies in the stomack, and that's not the place lime Nature hath provided to hold choler. Dame Nature is like a Prince in the body, and holds tenure by Soccage under Almighty God.
and if she can expel her enemy out of her dominions,
Doth she not do well ?

4. If together with what was mentioned before, there happen swelling or ringing by reason of wind under one of the sides, be not too hasty to predict vomiting; it is more probable to be only bleeding at the Nose.

5. Bleeding at the Nose in such a case usually happens to people under 30 years of age, vomiting to such as are older.

6. These presages hath HIPPOCRATES left to posterity, verified by his own experience: I have ordered them for your own good, as well as I can: I have given you the reasons of some of them, because I would instruct you; of

others I have not, because I would encourage you to study; for take this for an absolute truth, my writings may teach you, but it is your selves must make your selves Physitians. Doctor Reason told me these presages were true. And Experience tells you by my Pen, that you shall find them so. I now take my leave of you for this time, and withal tell you that if you be not so free to do good to others as I am to you, look to answer for it another day at the general account.

Infallible signes to discern of what Complexion any person is whatsoever.

The cholerick man for the most part is little, and short of stature; which hapneth (as I suppose) either by reason of the fewnesse of vapours and fumosities ingendered; or else, because that the radical moisture whereby the vertue nutritive and vegetable is sustained, is by the operation of strong heat and drinesse drawn to the centre, and there partly consumed; as fire (of whose nature is choler) attracteth moisture to itself, and drieth it up, so that the superficies and extream parts stretch not in length, neither wax big, or fat, because of defection of natural moisture, (as in aged persons in whom radical moisture is decayed) groweth no more: and his skin is rough and hot in touching, & his body very hair, their colour is betwixt yellow and red, with a certain glittering like fire; such persons soon have beards, and the colour of their hair is red, or auburn. As touching their conditions, they are naturally quick-witted, bold, unshamefac'd, furious, hasty, quarrelsome, ireful, fraudulent, stout, arrogant, couragious, gracelesse, cruel, crafty, and unconstant; light in moving, jesters, mockers, watchful, and flatterers, &c. their eyes little and hollow. Also the vertue of concoction in them is very strong, insomuch that he may digest more then he hath appetite for; his pulse is swift and strong, his urine yellow, and thin in substance; as touching their digestion, they are often costive, they dream of fire, fighting, and anger, of lightning, and dreadful apparitions of the air, by the means of hot and dry fumosities and vapours ascending from the stomack into the head, which trouble the brain and virtue imaginative.

Signs of cholerick melancholy man.

Cholerick melancholy men, are higher of stature then cholerick, because violent heat in them is more remisse and slack, whereby fumosities are the more ingendred, and radical moisture the lesse wasted; yet they are little and lean of body, because of drinesse, with skin rough and hard, meanly hairy, and temperate in feeling; their colour is palish, drawing towards a brimstone colour, for in it is seen a little skew of yellowishnesse; they have not beards so soon as cholerick men, and the colour of their hair is reddish, or light auburn- And touching the conditions, or natural inclination of such persons, they are not altogether so pregnant witted, bold, furious, quarrelsome, fraudulent, prodigal, stout, and couragious as cholerick men; neither so gracelesse, unconstant, flattering, swift, and scornful as they; yet they are suspitious, fretful, nigerdish, and more solitary, studious, and curious then cholerick and retain their anger longer. The vertue of digestion in such persons Is meetly strong, and their pulse lesser and slower then in cholerick persons; their Urine is yellow and thin, and they dream of falling from high places, of robberies, murders, harms proceeding of fire, fighting, anger and much like.

Signs of a Melancholy cholerick man.

Melancholy Cholerick men are tall of stature, by reason that natural heat is feeble, and thereby many fumosities are ingendered, but they are little and slender of body, because of drynesse, therefore their skin is rough and hard, and cold in touching: they have but very little hair on their bodies, and are long without beards, by means of cold which stopeth the Pores, and suffereth not the matter whereof hair is ingendered to come forth: Also they have much superfluity in the nose; their colour is pale, shaddowed with a little nigritude, or darknesse. And concerning their conditions, they are gentle, given to sobriety, solitary, studious, doubtful, avaritious, shamefac't, timerous, stubborn, fretful, pensive, constant, and true in action, with a deep surmise, and slow wit, with obliviousness; their hair is brown and thin, their digestion feeble, and less then their appetite, the pulse little and slack, their urine subcitrine and thin; and they dream of falling from high places, fearful dreams, and sundry varieties.

Signs of Melancholy men.

Melancholick men are mean of stature, .and seldome very tall; for excesse cold doth binde the substance, and suffreth it not to stretch in length; and although melancholy be dry in temperature, yet they are little, and slender of body, the occasion (I imagine) of excesse cold, by means whereof much superfluity is ingendered, which somewhat alayeth the drinesse, for melancholick men are full of Flegm, and rumatique matter. Their colour is duskish, and swartish pale, their skin is rough and cold in feeling; they have very little or no hair on their bodies, and are long without beards, yea, sometimes beardlesse; the colour of their hair is duskish; as touching their conditions, they are naturally covetous, self-lovers, fearfull without cause; pusillanimous, solitary, careful, lumpish, seldome merry or laughing, stout, stubborn, ambitious, envious, fretful, obstinate in opinions, of a deep cogitation, mistrustful, suspicious, vexed with dolours of the mind, and dreadful imaginations (as though they were infested with evil spirits) and are very spightful, curious, squeamish, and yet slovens, high-minded, and very majestical in behaviour, and retain their anger long; the vertue of concoction in them is very feeble; yet they have very good appetite to their meat. Their Urine is palish and mean in substance, and they dream of fearful things, terrible visions, and darknesse.

Signs of Melancholick sanguine man.

Melancholick sanguine men are higher of stature then melancholick; for in them natural heat is temperate; wherefore fumosities and radical moisture are meanly ingendered, whereby they are meanly big; fleshier, and firm of body; their colour is after a darkish red, their skin neither hard nor rough, but temperate in heat and softnesse, and not very hairy; they have beards about 21 years of age; and touching their conditions, they are more liberal, bolder, merrier, less stubborn, and not so pusillanous, solitary, and pensive, as melancholic persons, nor so vexed with dreadful imaginations as they are: also they are gentle, sober, patient, trusty, merciful, and affable; and to conclude, for as much as this complexion is temparate in quality, so likewise it is boon in conditions; for vertue is a mean between two extreams. Their urine is of light saffron colour, and mean in substance; their pulses are temperate in motion; they have pleasant dreams, and many times respondent to truth; and their digestion is meanly strong.

Signs of a Sanguine Melancholic man.

Sanguine Melancholick men are mean of stature, with bodies well compact with reins and arteries; fleshy, but not fat; they have skin meetly smooth, and hot in feeling, and are somewhat hairy, and, soon have beards; the colour of their hair is dark auburn, their cheeks red, shadowed with ?luteal colour. Their conditions are much like unto a sanguine mans, but they are not altogether so liberal, merry, and bold, for they have as it were a spice of the inclination of melancholy persons. Their pulses are great and full, urine yellow and mean in substance, with dreaming of deep pits, wells, and such like; their digestion is indifferent.

Signs of a Sanguine man.

Sanguine men are of a mean form, their bodies well composed, with larger limbs, and fleshier, but not fat; with great veins and arteries, smooth skins, hot and moist in feeling, the body hairy, and soon bearded; their colour is white, intermixed with redness in the cheeks; their hair for the most part is brown. And touching their conditions, they are merry, liberal, bountiful, courteous, bold enough, merciful, trusty, faithful, and of good behaviour; a little thing will cause him to weep, and when that is done, no further grief sticketh to their hearts; which is contrary to melancholy men, for they cannot weep, although it be in a matter that concerns them neer, but yet their cogitation thereof is imprinted in their hearts. The sanguine man hath good appetite, and quick digestion; his urine is yellow and thick, his pulse great and full, and dreameth of red things, and pleasant conceits.

Signs of a Sanguine phlegmatick man.
Sanguine phlegmatique men are higher of stature then Sanguine, because more superfluities are ingendered in their bodies, and are of substance much like unto Sanguine; their hair is flaxen, or light auburn, their colour is like red, but not intermixed as Sanguine are; as touching their

conditions, they are less ,liberal, sadder, and not so bold as Sanguine are,_not so hairy; their urine is subcitrine, and mean in substance, their pulses moderate, with good appetite, and digestion indifferent; they dream of flying in the air, and falling down from some mountain, or high place into water, or such like.

Signs of a Phlegmatique Sanguine man.

Phlegmatic Sanguine men are mean of stature, and somewhat grosse of body, with a smooth and soft skin, and cold in touching; their bodies are hairy, and long without beards; their hair is light yellow, or flaxen, plain and smooth; their colour is neither white nor red, but mean between both; of conditions, neither very merry, nor much sad; not liberal, or covetous; not much bold, not very fearful, &c. The vertue of digestion in them is somewhat slack, and lesser then their appetite, their pulses are low and little, with dreaming of sundry fables.

Signs of a Phlegmatick man

Phlegmatic men are shorter of stature, for although much vapours and superfluity is ingendered in their bodies, yet by means of coldness the substance is bound and staid from stretching in length; nevertheless moisture dealith itself in breadth, and maketh them grosse and fat. Their veins and arteries are small, their bodies without hair; they have little beards, and their hair is flaxen; their colour whitish, with smooth skin, and cold in touching; As concerning their conditions, they are very dull, heavy, sloathful, sleepy, cowardish, fearful, covetous, self-lovers, slow of motion, shamefac.d, and sober. In them the vertue of digestion and appetite is feeble, (through defect of natural heat) their pulses are little and slow, and their urine pale and thick; with dreaming of water, &c.

Signs of a Phlegmatick Cholerick man.

Cholerick-phlegmatick

Phlegmatick cholerick men are tall of stature, and not so big and fat as phlegmatick, and are more hairy, and sooner have beards; their hair is light auburn, in which some shew of yellow, and are temperate in feeling; And touching their conditions, they are nimbler, bolder, and kinder then phlegmatick, and are not so drowsie, and sluggish as they are, but merrier, and quicker witted; Their face for the most part is full of freckles, and their colour white, shadowed with yellowishnesse: their appetite and digestion is indifferent; their pulses are moderate and full, their urine subcitrine and meane in substance, dreaming of swimming water, or snow or rain.

Signes of a Cholerick phlegmatick man.

Cholerick phlegmatick men are meane of stature, firm, and strong of body, and neither fat nor lean, with great legs, and their skin hairy, and moderate in feeling, their hair is yellowish, and their colour the same; their conditions are not much different from cholerick men, but they are not altogether so furious and bold as they, neither so prodigal, and guileful; for flegm doth somewhat allay the heat of choler; their digestion is perfect, their pulse swift, and their urine like Saffron and thin, with dreaming of battels, strife, lightning, and hot water.

URINALIA:

or

A Treatise of the CRISIS hapning to the Urine

Through default either of the
Reins, Bladder, Yard, Conduits
or Passages

*With their Causes, Signs
and Cures*

BY
NICHOLAS CULPEPER
Student in *Physick*
and *Astrology*
London

Printed for Nath. Brook, at the Angel
in Cornhil, 1658.

My one child being annoyed with one of these Diseases about the year 1645 made me set and fix my studies upon this subject, the method of which will appear by this Table.

A Table of the Diseases handled in this Treatise.

Chapter 1

Of pissing Blood.

It is caused in divers ways:

1. Through weaknesse of the reins.
2. Through dissolution of the VENA CAVA.
3. Through over-lifting, or some fall, whereby some vein in the reins is broken.
4. Through sharp humours, that cause excoriation.
5. Through stopping of. the Hemerrhoids.

If this disease be caused through weaknesse of the reins, the blood that comes out looks wheyish.

If of a breaking vein, the blood comes out abundantly, with great weakness of the back.

But if it proceed of corrosion, it comes forth little by little, with vehement pain in the reins.

If it proceed of weaknesse of the reins, or dissolution of the VENA CAVA, you must use retrictive medicines.

Abstain from such things as provoke Urine; and

from venery.

For Simples: Comfrey-roots, Gum tracacanth, **and Arabick, Lapis Haematites, Willow-leaves,** juyce of Knotgrasse; and above all the herb of VENUS, called VERVAIN gathered in the hour of VENUS, when the MOON is with her in LIBRA, is medicinal for all diseases in the reins.

For compounds, Trochysks of Amber; of Terre lemnia, of Spodium, those called Gordonii; Syrup made with Sugar, and the juyce of Marygolds, Pomegranat-rinds, and flowers; the leaves of Oak, Mirtle berries, &c.

It if proceed of a vein that is broken, you must presently let blood on the arm of the same side, that the blood may be turned; then keep the region of the Reins moist with oyl of Roses, and Vinegar, using the former Medicines.

But if it come by excoriation caused by corroding humours, purge out the humours first.

But by all means keep him from all salt, sharp, and soure things, for they cause humours that increase the corrosion.

Other medicines for this you may find in that Chapter which treats of ulcerations in the reins.

Yet note, that in pissing blood, coming of what cause soever, it profiteth much to drink new milk in abundance, and no other drink but that.

Chapter II.
Of Inflammations in the Reins.

It is caused either through corruption of humours, or stripes, or drinking of medicines that cause inflammation, or through continual and vehement riding.

There chanceth to them that labour of this disease, a beating pain in the small of the back, a little above the bastard ribs, which extendeth it self downward, to the hips, bladder, and privities, an astonishment in the legs, difficulty to go; and if they chance to sneeze, they are vexed with vehement pain.

There followeth also difficulty of urine, they pisse often and painfully.

The calves of the legs and feet are cold, they cannot stop without great pain; their urine is grosse and filthy, and their body feverish. Some have a pronesse to vomit, and some do vomit choler; some are troubled with belchings, some sweat, and some faint.

But all are exceedingly troubled with wind, and abhor meat.

Let the sick abstain from all hot, bitter, and gnawing or salt meats.

This disease hapneth most to women with child.

Herbs medicinal are Endive, Cichory, Lettice, Plantan, Purslain, Water-lillies, House-leek, and night shade.

Let them lodge in a soft bed.

Let them abhor feasting, for fasting causeth sharpnesse of urine.

Also an emulsion made with the four greater cold feeds. White Poppy-seeds, Almonds, Plantain water, and Sugar profiteth much.

Also Cinammon profiteth much used any way; and so doth Mallows.

Those women with child that are troubled with it, are always troubled with an extream bearing down, as though the child were misplaced; their labours are tedious, as by reason of the heat of the reins they easily suffer abortion, and continually fall in labour long before their time.

My own wife hath in every child been extreamly perplexed with this disease, yet I never knew the cause of it before the writing hereof.

In cure of this disease you must avoid all medicines that provoke urine.

Nourish the region of the reins with any or all the Oyls (I mean not Chymical Oyls, but Oyls made by the decoction of the herb in Oyl) of the herbs afore-mentioned.

If men be troubled with it, you may see **blood** freely without fear, for that cools the **blood**, and makes lesse of it; but blood-letting in women with child takes away the nourishment of the child, and causeth abortion.

In fine, let them drink two ounces of the juyce of Clary, and as much juyce of Nightshade in six ounces of stale Ale, morning and evening.

Chapter III.
Of the Stone in the Reins.

The Stone in the Reins hapneth oftner to men of perfect age then to children. It is caused of continual crudities and rawness of the stomach, whereby abundance of grosse and earthy humours are gathered together, which the fiery heat about the reins parcheth and hardneth like a stone.

The stones that be in the reins near the ventricles, differ amongst themselves in greatnesse, fashion, sharpness, and colour; for some are black, some white, and some of a pale or ashy colour.

The sick of this disease have a fore pain in the reins of the back, pricking as though an Aul were thrust in; yet no swelling appears outwardly; he can hardly move his back at all, the leg that is next the diseased side is so benumbed; They loath their meat, and are subject to vomiting; their urine either is very little in quantity, or else quite stopped.

They have many motions to stool, and yet are astringent, also the urine hath a gravelly residence.

If the party be young and full of blood, you may breath a vein, otherwise forbear.

But however forget not to purge the grosse melancholick humours with black Hellebore, corrected with Cinamon, of LIGNUM CASSIAE.

If strength be very weak, and the Patient by reason of age or other impediment, not fit for purgation, you must keep his body solluble; with gently Clysters, in which put oyl of Rew, Dill, Chamomel, &c.

Keep the region of the reins always anointed with oyl of Chamomel, over which apply a Tobacco leaf warmed, and change twice in 24 hours.

The best medicine ever I read or heard of, for this disease, is to drink the juice of Pellitory of the wall every morning.

Neither do I believe the juyce of Chamomel is much inferiour to it.

Powders medicinal for this disease are, The seeds of Ammi, Gromwel, Marsh-mallows; the roots of Marsh-mallows, Sparagus, Fennel, Parsley, Bruscus-Saxifrage, Filipendula, Aristolochia rotunda, Mather, the herbs of Pellitory of the wall, Marsh-mallows, Mallows, Chammomel, Folymountain, Peniroyal.

Cinamon, Bdellium, Winter-cherries, Gum of Plum trees, Holly-berries, the stones of Sea-Sponges, lapis Judaicus.

Boyl those that are to be boyled, and beat the rest into a powder and give it.

Moreover these stones are often brought by force of medicine from the reins, and yet stick at the neck of the bladder, stop the urine, prick by their own sharpnesse, and so put the Patient to worse torture then before.

In such cases you must first let out the urine with an Instrument.

Then you must labour to break the stone in the bladder, with such medicines as you shall find in the Chapter of the stone in the bladder.

Again, sometimes the stone passeth the neck of the bladder, and yet stiketh in the midst of the Yard, and sometimes causeth exulceration there too.

In such cases you must hold the Yard in Oyl of Chamomel as hot as can be endured.

The best way to make Oyl of Chamomel for such uses, is to boyl the juyce of Chamomel, first clarified, with the like quantity of Saller-oyl, till the juyce be consumed.

If by this means, and his straining hard to pisse, it be not expelled, you have no other way but to use incision.

Which must be made on the upper part of the yard through the glans, and draw it out through the incision with an instrument.

For if you make the incision in the lower part of the yard, it always fistulates, and the urine comes out there.

After the Patient is whole, let him use preservatives which may keep him from the like again, for commonly the disease often returns.

Let him chew his meat well; but let him eat but little corn, cheese, nor milk, nor of anything that is made of them.

Let him avoid fish, all wines but white wines, all meats of bad juyce, and hard of digestion.

Let him not eat much at one time, and that which he doth let it be quick of digestion.

Let him often drink wormwood-beer.

Parsnips are exceeding good food for him, so are most of the herbs mentioned in the cure; with the roots and seeds.

If blood abounds, breath a vein.

If vicious humours draw together, use a purge which fits their temperature.

Chapter IV
Of unmeasurable pissing

There is a disease in the reins, wherein whatsoever is drunk, is presently pissed out again.

It is caused by reason of weaknesse of the retentive vertue of the reins, and the attractive draws freely without control.

There accompanies this disease an immoderate heat all over the body; a stubborn desire to drink; neither is their thirst quenched by drinking.

There always is a Fever accompanying this disease;and the whole body wasteth, consumeth, and penth away.

The cure consisteth in two things:
1 To stop the sharpnesse of the humours.
2 To correct the retentive faculty of the reins.
Therefore it is a laudable remedy often to-cause them to
vomit up again what they leave drunk.

Let his diet be things that want mordacity, or gnawing,
and provoke no urine; such be eggs, lean swines flesh,
much sodden, new cheese without salt, milk wherein
Flint-stones, or red-hot steel hath been quenched.

Yet if the Patient be astringent, as my own daughter
was, (for under this disease she laboured a long time, and
went not to stool all the time without compulsion) you must
avoid the latter, for it causeth astringency.

For Pot-herbs, use Endive, Chicory, Lettice, Purslane,
&c.

Medicinal for the disease, are Knotgrasse, Bloodwort,
the juyce of them, if it may be had, Comfrey, Dates,
Mirtle-berries, Pears used in decoctions, Trochisiks of
Spodium.

Also sweet wines are very medicinal to drink, for it
changeth the salt humours which cause thirst, and makes
the blood and humours sweet.

That which I found most benefit by in my daughter's
sicknesse, was by applying Alhoof chopped small, not
washed at all, sprinkled with a little white wine-vinegar,
and applied to her wrist.

Also three holly leaves boyled in white wine for her to
drink.

And these I leaned of an Italian.

Also these things are good to anoint the reins, Red
rose-vinegar, Nightshade, Lettice, Ducks-meat, Pellitory of
the wall, Purslane, &c. boyled in Oyl of Roses, or Mirtles.

Chapter V

Of Ulcers in the Reins.

They are caused either of rupture of some **veins in their reins, or through some inflalion there, or through** sharp humours carried thither, which causeth excoriation.

There is in this disease pain and heaviness felt in the loins, the urine comes forth without any impediment, and thereby it is known from ulcers in the bladder.

Also there is matter pissed out with the urine, and sometimes hairs; and take it for a general maxim, if mattery stuff is pissed out with the urine there is an ulcer; if the urine come with much pain, the ulcer is in the bladder; if not it is in the reins.

Let the sick eschew crudities, fatiety, and fulness, all raw meats that speedily turn to putrefaction, or that cause inflammation or windinesse.

Let him avoid all salt, soure, and sharp things, all things that ingender choler, such be much thirst, abstinence, hunger, labour, wrath, watching, &c.

He must above all things avoid violent motions, ridings, as also perpetual idlenesse.

Let his bread be new, and not leavened.

Let his meat be light of digestion, and of good juyce, such as Chicken, Lamb, young Rabbits, Birds of the mountains, &c.

Also milk sodden with eggs, and thickened with white starch is very good.

But above all, and before all other medicines, you must be sure to cleanse the reins well, else your going about to cure them is but a labour in vain.

That you may do it by pil. Mastichine, or pil. de Succino, if the putrefaction be not great: if it be you must use a drying diet composed of Cuajacu hermodactiles, Senna, Epithimu, Stechas, Aniseeds.

Which lest it should cause inflammation by its heat; you may add to it cooling and slippery herbs, as Mallows. Mars-mallows roots and leaves, Endive, Chicory, &c.

After you may administer such medicines as stop gnawing, and corrhoding humours, such be Endive, Sorrel,

Lettice, Purslane; the four greater cold Sweds, Fenugreek seeds boyled in Honey.

Also let him drink much Honey and Milk for Honey cleanseth Ulcers exceedingly.

Let him by all means avoid all cold drinks, for cold is an enemy to Ulcers.

Let him use Emulsions made with Almonds, and cold seeds, Gum Tracanth, Arabick, and Barley-water.

The reins being well cleansed, you may come to restrictives.

Such be bole-Armeniack, Dragons blood, gu. Arabick, and Tracanth, Terra-Lemnia, White-starch, Spodium, &c.

Also outwardly you may strengthen the place with Oyl of Roses, Mirtles, Frankincense, Mastick, &c.

Chapter VI
Of the Stone in the Bladder.

The Stone in the Bladder ingendereth oftner in children, then in old people.

It is caused by abundance of grosse and thick urine, carried into the bladder, and feeling there, like the lecs of Wine, is compacted together and hardned into a stone; by the heat of the Bladder, and Parts adjacent.

Those that have this disease, their privy members itch much, they handle them often, many times they swell; they make water often, and by drops, and their water is gravelly; also they feele a weight or nearing down about their fundament.

Let their body be kept soluble.

Besides the things mentioned in the chapter of the stone in the reines, the approved remedy is a Hedg-sparrow killed in the right time (I shall God willing hereafter write a Treatise of the true refer you for this:) and salted up, **and eaten raw for this disease, which will break and bring away the hardest stone that can be** away the hardest stone that can be in the body of man.

Also the juyce of Chamomel, cast up into the bladder with a spring, will break the stone, and bring it away speedily.

The like effect hath Goats blood taken inwardly.

Sometimes the stone rusheth into the neck of the bladder, and stops by that means the urine; in such cases you must place the patient in his bed so, as lying on his back his privities may be highest, and then remove the stone with an instrument.

Thus you have waies enough for the cure of the stone without cutting, which is a medicine invented rather to kill then cure the diseased.

Chapter VII
Of blood curdled in the bladder.

If a veine chance to break in the bladder, as sometimes doth, then the blood that falls out of it into the bladder thickens and curdles.

In such cases the patients heart failes him, his visage waxeth pale, his pulses are small, deep and thick; he is sorrowful, cold, and his strength decayes.

Also sometimes a clod of blood happneth into the passage of the urine and stoppeth it. In all Breaking out of blood you must be speedy in your cure as you can; delayes are dangerous. And therefore in this.

If strength and age permit, let blood presently, let blood often, and but little at a time, for that turns the blood and draws it back.

Boyle Knotgrasse, plantane, Bramble leaves, Comfry, and Pomgranat flowers, in water and vinegar, of each a like quantity, and wet cloaths and foment the region of the bladder often, and let a stupe made of Bais lie alwzies wet to the place.

Inwardly, the foregoing hearbs, as also Motherwort, Stoechas, Citron pils, Wormwood, Southernwood,

Calaminth, Elder-leaves, Bitumen, Jodiacum, Gum
Ammoniacum, and Spermacetu are medicinal.

If the clotted blood stops the passage of the urine, you
must bring out the urine with a Syringe, as in the stone.

Chapter VIII
Inflammation of the Bladder.

Of all diseases in the bladder this is the most grievous
and deadly.

There followeth this disease a sharp feaver, they rave
and cannot sleep, and talk they know not what.

Their urine is stopped, sometimes the vomit pure
choler.

Their groyne is hard, and vehemently pained, they
have a desire to go to stoole, yet many times they can do
nothing, as it happens in the disease Tenasmus.

Those that have this disease, if strength and age permit,
bleed them instantly in the ankles. Let them abstaine from
all meate and broaths made of meat.

Let his drink be only water in which barley and
cinnamon are sodden.

Let all cold things be avoyded, for the bladder is full of
sinews, and all cold is an enemy to the sinews.

You must refresh the region of the Bladder with oyl
wherein Dill and Linseed hath been boyled. Avoid by all
means all medicines that coole and bind, for they prohibit
the dissolving of those humours that cause the
inflammation.

Let the **guts be alwaies** kept washed with gentle and
soft clysters.

Then boyle White Poppyshells in oyle, and mingle
Saffron, Myrrhe, and Opium, with the Oyle, **being stained,
and** wet a little wool in it, and put this up the fundament
when the clister is come away. This continue during the
sicknesse. Also you may boyl Linseed, Fenugreek seed, and

Marsh-mallows leaves, and roots, and put it, liquor and all into a close stoole, and let the Patient sit with his fundament over the steme of it.

Let him abstain from much drink, and all things that provide urine, or cause sharpnesse of urine.

Also if urgent occasion be, you may bind the extream parts hard.

Some use cupping-glasses, but I never knew them do good but harm.

Chapter IX
Of Ulcers in the Bladder

Ulcers happen in the bladder either by some boyle or botch which hath hapned before, or through some rupture and gnawing flux from the reines.

There followeth this disease, a sharp pain in the bladder, pissing of matter and filth with their urine, and making water with great difficulty, and it stinketh abominably.

If the ulcer lie in the bottom of the bladder, then there is pain about the groyn, but if in the neck of the bladder, the pain is most extream when he maketh water, both in the beginning and end of his pissing.

They desire to sit stooping forward continually, and cannot stand upright, nor rest, lying along, but are troubled with continual watchings, and consumings of body, and it many times brings them to a fever, and so kills them.

I cured two of this disease, and I hold it to be the most difficult disease to cure that is, none excepted, and that for these reasons:

First, the bladder is mighty full of sinews; and ulcers are difficult to cure, when they happen in sinewie places.

Secondly, because of the great remotenesse of the place; the medicine must pass two concoctions, besides the reines and kidneys, before it can come to the bladder, & so the natural strength of it is wel nigh spent before it can come to do its office in the least measure.

Thirdly, the bladder is a place appropriated onely to keep excrements, and therefore the excrement of the medicine onely is permitted to come thither.

Fourthly, because the urine, which is by nature sharp, doth continually touch the ulcers, and gnaweth them, and thereby keepeth them from conglutination or joyning together.

For when never so much urine is sent out some will remain behind, and the bladder shrinketh up, and falleth together, so that the urine which is left, toucheth every part of the bladder, yea although it be never so little.

For the cure then of this dangerous and difficult disease, in the first place perswade the patient to drinke nothing but new milke, and abundance of it, for it alone in time will cure him.

Also cast new milke and oyle of roses into the bladder with a syringe.

For other medicines seeke them in the chapter of the Ulcers in the reines.

Chapter X.
Of the Strangury

This disease is called in Latin STILLIVIDIUM URINAE, in English the Strangury.

It is a disease wherein the urine distilleth down little by little, by drops, and cause the a continual provocation and desire to pisse.

It is caused either through the sharpnesse of the urine, or by exulcerations of the bladder, or by imposthumation of the liver or reines, whereby filth and matter is sent into the bladder, the sharpnesse of which causeth a continual desire to pisse.

You may known if comes by sharpness of the urine, by the cholleriquenes of the urine; also, gnawing about the bladder, and the whole state of the body shews choler to abound.

If by ulceration of the bladder or reines, the former Chapters will direct you.

If it be caused through sharpnesse of humours, you must purge out the vicious humour with all speed.

Cassia fistula is a delicate purge for this purpose; so is Lenitive Electuary, an ounce of either, taken at night going to bed.

Let his diet be moistning and let him drink warm milk.

Let him pisse continually, for the sharpnesse of the urine will ulcerate the bladder if it abide long in it.

For simples, Marsh-mallow leaves and roots, the roots of Philipendula, and Osmund royal, Gromwel seed, and winter Cherries, are medicinal.

To mitigate the sharpnesse of the urine, you may cast in milk mingled with white starch, with a Syringe.

If it come of ulcers in the bladder, you must cure them, and then the strangury will cease.

Chapter XI
Of difficulty of Urine.

Dysury is a disease wherein the urine is made with great difficulty and hardnesse.

It is caused through great weaknesse or coldnesse of the bladder, or through a flegmatique humour that stoppeth the neck of the bladder.

You may know if it come of cold, by the whitenesse of the urine; if of flegmatique humours by the thicknesse of the urine; however it comes away with no final pain.

If it come of coldnesse in the bladder, use hot things that are diverticks. Such be Crabs, and Hedghogs dried, the flesh of them I mean. Diacalaminthes, Diacurcuma, Fennel, Parsl.ey, Smallage, with many others which you may finde in my volume of hearbs and roots.

If it proceed of flegmatique humours, first purge flegme with Ocymel scilliticum.

Besides the former medicines you may strengthen the region of the bladder with Oyles of Rew, Dill, Scorpions, Castroreum, Chamomel, Southernwood, Bettony, Mugwort, Calaminth, any of these, CONSIDERATIS CONSIDERANDIS.

Also you may make a Nodulus with any of these oyles, and put up the fundament.

Chapter XII
Of stoppage in the Urine.

SUPRESSIO URINE in Latin, is a disease wherein the urine is totally letted and stopped, so that the Patient cannot pisse at all.

This disease is caused either through weakness of the bladder, or by the stopping the passage of the urine, either by a material stone, or by gross humours, or by some swelling in the passage, or by inflammation which stops the passage; and sometimes a little piece of flesh or hard knob grows, in the passage, and sometimes matter sent down from the reins stops the passage and sometimes this disease chanceth to hail folk, only through long retention of their urine.

If it come through weaknesse of the bladder we skewed the signes in the former chapter.

If of grosse humours, it may be known by the diet the Patient kept, as idle life, feeding on gross meats, &c.

If by inflammation or stone, &c. you may find the signs in their proper chapters, and their cure also.

If it be caused of some piece of flesh growing there, it carries the same sign with ulcers in the reins, also a syringe put in the urine comes out; also the piece of flesh being touched with the Syrenge, causeth pain, whereby you may know whereabout it lies; also by breaking it pieces of flesh come out with the urine, and blood also.

180

If it come of clotted blood, there went before it pissing of blood.

If it comes of matter, there went before it the running of the reines.

The cure is diverse, according to the diversity of the causes.

If it come of weaknesse of the bladder, nourish the bladder with hot Oyles mentioned in the former Chapter. If of a knob of flesh you are furnished with medicines in the chapter of the stone in the reines.

The other cures may be found in the precedent chapters. Generally all things provoking urine are medicinal for this disease.

Chapter XIII
Of Ulcers in the Yard.

Ulcers are bred in the Yard through the sharpnesse of the humour in the running of the reines, and they come alwaies with inflammation.

They are then cured by injections made with TROCHISCI ALBI RHAZIS CUM OPIO. DRACH. l- Plantan water oun. 4 mixed together, and cast in with a Syringe.

Sometimes they are caused by gravel, which causeth excoriation in the Yard. They they are best cured by drying medicines.

Such be Paper burnt, Dill burnt, Aristolochia rotunda, Mirrhe, Galls, Cum Arabick, Dragons blood, Bole Armenick, Putty, Lapis Haematitis, Terre Jemnia. These or any of these CONSIDERATIS CONSIDERANDIS.

If the exulceration be foule, you may first cleanse it with water and honey.

Also outwardly you may apply a cloath dipt in water of Roses, Houseleek, or Nightshade.

FINIS

Felix quis potuit rerum cognoscere causas.

Vale.   N. CULPEPER